Comparative Politics
by Dankwart Rustow

Congress and the Presidency
by Nelson W. Polsby

International Relations
by Karl Deutsch

Modern Political Analysis
by Robert A. Dahl

Perspectives in Constitutional Law
by Charles Black

Politics and Policies in State and Local Governments
by Herbert Kaufman

Public Administration
by James Fesler

Public Opinion and Ideology
by Robert E. Lane and David Sears

The Age of Ideology—Political Thought, 1750 to the Present
by Frederick M. Watkins

The American Party System and the American People
by Fred I. Greenstein

Readings in American Political Behavior
edited by Raymond E. Wolfinger

FOUNDATIONS OF MODERN POLITICAL SCIENCE SERIES
Robert A. Dahl, Editor

Politics
and Policies
in
State and Local
Governments

FOUNDATIONS OF MODERN POLITICAL SCIENCE SERIES

ENGLEWOOD CLIFFS, NEW JERSEY   Prentice-Hall, Inc.

HERBERT KAUFMAN

Yale University

(

218917 ACLS

POLITICS AND POLICIES IN STATE AND LOCAL GOVERNMENTS

by *Herbert Kaufman*. © *Copyright 1963 by* PRENTICE-HALL, INC.,

Englewood Cliffs, New Jersey.   All rights reserved. No part of this book may

be reproduced in any form, by mimeograph or any other means, without per-

mission in writing from the publishers. Printed in the United States of America.

Library of Congress Catalog Card No.: 63–11093. Design by Walter Behnke

FOUNDATIONS OF MODERN POLITICAL SCIENCE SERIES

Robert A. Dahl, Editor

c

Preface

A reader who accepts at face value everything
in this book—in *any* book, for that matter—will have missed
its main point. I hope to stimulate thought, not
to suppress it; to raise questions,
not to pronounce dogma; to suggest answers and ways
of getting answers, not to set down formulae.
I do not mean the substantive discussion
is factually inaccurate. Nor is it, despite its relative brevity,
incomplete. But the way facts are ordered, and inferences
drawn from them, is a product
of the perspectives and values of authors.
I do not refer simply to "liberal" and "conservative"
prejudices. I mean also the determination of what
is worth examining and what may safely
be ignored; the interpretation of the way

the system works, who benefits from it, and who is disadvantaged; the assessment of the direction of development and of the consequences. All these are functions of an author's orientation, and the alert reader will constantly challenge, demand evidence, and test arguments against his own experience instead of accepting them passively.

Thus, for example, in discussing the division of functions among the levels of government, I have stressed the dimensions of the responsibilities assumed by state and local governments rather than, as is so often the case these days, the impact of grants-in-aid. I have made judgments about differences between urban and non-urban forms of politics and predictions about the future of government in metropolitan areas. The political processes of states and communities are represented as remarkably open even to minorities, not as dominated by unified political elites. The design of governmental machinery is interpreted in terms of a quest for specified values. These and many other assertions may be viewed as hypotheses to be investigated and evaluated rather than as ultimate truths.

In other words, this book is intended as a point of departure, not as the last word. Every meaningful examination of political processes ought to be an exercise in political theory at some level. Whether or not this book meets this test, it can best serve its purpose if its readers approach it in this spirit.

I took advantage of many friends in the course of writing this book, but to none am I more heavily indebted than to Robert V. Presthus and Duane Lockard, who offered detailed comments on, and criticisms of, the entire manuscript. Fred I. Greenstein, Norman Rubin, Clement E. Vose, and Robert C. Wood addressed themselves to particular parts of the manuscript, and their advice saved me from many errors. While I have no desire to share with anyone such praise as this volume may elicit, I am compelled to admit that its virtues would be fewer had not these commentators been so generous with their assistance. And while I have no wish to absolve them of all responsibility for the book's faults, I must confess I was not always able to follow their advice. I am thus forced to share what I would rather keep for myself, and to shoulder alone what I would much prefer to share.

For constructive editorial advice and help I owe a great deal to Alfred Goodyear, James Murray, and Wilbur Mangas of Prentice-Hall. In the preparation of the manuscript for the printer, I was greatly aided by the efforts of Ruth L. Davis, Joy du Trieuille, and Gordon E. Pruett.

To my students of state and local government at Yale I owe a great deal for providing the stimulus of a sympathetic and tolerant but intelligently and constructively critical audience. For me, this association has been highly fruitful as well as pleasant, and I am happy to have this chance to thank them publicly.

Herbert Kaufman.

New Haven
1963

Preface

Contents

Contents

A Family of Governments

C H A P T E R   O N E

People in other parts of the world often find American
government and politics baffling, if not downright mysterious,
and Americans who try to explain our system
to them frequently find the experience frustrating. This mutual
unintelligibility is partly explained by the unique setting in which
our governmental and political system functions: the richness
and variety of our land, the conquest of the continent by immigrants
from all over the world, the commitment to operate
through private organizations rather than public institutions,

1

the absence of a rigid class structure, the relative isolation of the country during the period in which its political practices took shape, the orientation of its massive technology toward the satisfaction of consumer demands and the consequent extraordinary rise in its standards of living, the nation's recent and sudden emergence as a world leader, and many other factors that would make America different even if its governmental structure and processes were much the same as those of other countries.

In addition, however, its governmental structure and processes are distinctive. In a real sense, America does not have a single government, but a family of governments. (See Table 1.) No one can understand the

Table 1   GOVERNMENTAL UNITS IN THE UNITED STATES

Type of Government	Number of Units		
	1957[b]	1952[a]	1942[a]
Total	102,392	116,743	155,116
U.S. government	1	1	1
States	50	48	48
Counties	3,050	3,049	3,050
Municipalities	17,215	16,778	16,220
Townships & towns	17,198	17,202	18,919
School districts	50,454	56,346	108,579
Special districts	14,424	12,319	8,299

[a] Alaska, Hawaii, Puerto Rico, and their subdivisions are not included in these figures.
[b] Alaska and Hawaii and their subdivisions are included, but not Puerto Rico.
Sources: U.S. Bureau of the Census, 1957 Census of Governments, Vol. I, No. 1, Governments in the United States, p. 1; Statistical Abstract of the United States, 1961 (82nd ed.; Washington, 1961) p. 401.

United States who does not understand and appreciate this central characteristic of our system.

States, Localities, and the National Government

STATES, LOCALITIES, AND CONGRESS

It is easy for a foreign observer, accustomed to thinking of "Washington" as though it were a monolithic unit, familiar with the highly disciplined parties of his own country, and projecting onto the United States the image of rigorously subordinated sub-national governments acquired from his experience at home, to underestimate grossly the importance of the American states and their subdivisions in the national government. It is especially easy for someone unacquainted with the details of congressional behavior to overlook or dismiss the identification of senators and representatives with their constituencies—an identification springing sometimes from their conceptions of their functions as elected spokesmen, sometimes from interests they share with constituents, sometimes from acute sensitivity to the requirements of political survival, but an identification that expresses itself in their official actions over and over again whatever its source. Nobody who studies Congress at all can long remain unaware of the deep and unremitting consciousness of senators and representatives

2

that they speak for their respective areas, an obligation widely regarded as justly taking priority over party solidarity except in critical cases. Indeed, some students of American government deplore the narrowness of legislators' perspectives and voice concern about the sacrifice of national interests (however these may be defined) to local interests. No matter what a person feels about the *desirability* of this state of affairs, regardless of how "statesmanlike" members of Congress may be, they never cease to be delegates of the states and localities in which they are chosen.

Moreover, state legislatures help determine the composition of Congress. In the first place, although Congress determines the number of representatives to be allotted to each state, the boundaries of their districts are established by state legislation.[1] Since the rural areas of many states are overrepresented in state legislatures compared to the urban-suburban complexes of metropolitical regions (i.e., the rural proportion of the state legislatures is far greater than the rural proportion of the total state populations), state legislatures have tended to draw the boundaries of congressional districts in such a way as to strengthen rural representation in Congress.[2] As a result, bills dealing with social and economic welfare, housing, urban renewal, and even foreign aid have had heavy sledding in Congress, whereas price supports for farm products, and other forms of subsidies to farmers and food industries, have been favored; policies are affected by the composition of legislative bodies. Given its present composition, Congress is unlikely to correct the imbalance. Thus, if metropolitan residents want greater influence in Congress in order to secure more sympathetic treatment of urban-oriented legislation, they will probably have to begin by improving their position in the state legislatures.[3] In other words, you

[1] The Constitution of the United States assigns to the state legislatures the authority to prescribe "the Times, Places, and Manner of holding Elections for Senators and Representatives," but authorizes Congress "at any time [to] make or alter such regulations" (Article I, Section 4). Although Congress has legislated on its own election, it has left considerable discretion over federal elections to the states. The total number of representatives is set by law, and the apportionment of seats to each state is handled more or less automatically by the Bureau of the Census under statutory authorization and guidance. The drawing of congressional district boundaries, however, has been left by Congress to the state legislatures.

If a state fails to provide for new districts after a change in the size of its congressional delegation, following a census, Congress has directed by law that *all* such a state's representatives shall be elected at large. Sometimes states that gain representatives opt to elect the additional ones at large in order to avoid the bitter battles that full-scale redistricting frequently entails; electing the *new* representatives at large permits such states to retain their old district lines for all their other representatives. This practice has not been successfully challenged in the courts or in Congress. All in all, then, the boundaries of representatives' constituencies are set by the states for all practical purposes.

[2] That is, although every congressional district is represented by a single member of the House of Representatives, the districts in rural sections are often very sparsely populated, whereas districts in urban sections are commonly very heavily populated. Similar disparities—indeed, more pronounced disparities—occur also in many state legislative districts. See Gordon E. Baker, *Rural versus Urban Political Power* (Garden City,. N.Y.: Doubleday, 1955), especially chapters III and V; and Paul T. David and Ralph Eisenberg, *Devaluation of the Urban and Suburban Vote* (Charlottesville, Va.: Bureau of Public Administration, University of Virginia, 1961).

[3] In their struggle, metropolitan residents turned to the federal courts for help. For many years, however, the Supreme Court resolutely refused to accept suits challenging the fairness of the boundaries of state legislative districts (South v. Peters,

3

cannot understand Congress and what Congress does unless you understand the politics of states and localities.

The influence that states and localities exert on congressional composition is further magnified by state legislative control of eligibility to vote in party primaries and in all general elections (including federal elections), subject only to the broad voting provisions of the United States Constitution and to relatively limited federal statutes.[4] In the South this power has been used to prevent or discourage voting by Negroes, so that southern senators and representatives have been able to ignore without fear of political disadvantage the desires and aspirations of the Negro community. What is more, southern members of Congress exercise considerable influence, because committee chairmanships are allocated on a seniority basis, and the one-party monopoly in southern states projects them into positions of leadership whenever the Democrats control Congress.[5] The effects of these situations on all bills involving civil rights and prohibition of discrimination are obvious. Beyond these effects, however, such condi-

---

339 U.S. 279 (1950)) or of congressional districts (Colegrove v. Green, 328 U.S. 549 (1946)), holding this issue to be political rather than justiciable. Then, in 1962, the Supreme Court departed from this tradition and held that the fairness of state legislative districting *is* justiciable, since unfair districts might contravene the "equal protection of the laws" clause of the Fourteenth Amendment (Baker v. Carr, 179 F. Supp. 824 (1962)). The full impact of this decision may not be felt for some time, but the long-run consequences could be sweeping.

This decision may render unnecessary the quest for an amendment to the Constitution of the United States to compel more equitable representation in state legislatures. In 1960, and again in 1961, Senator Joseph S. Clark of Pennsylvania introduced such a measure, but no action was taken.

[4] Article I, Section 2, of the Constitution of the United States provides that "the electors [i.e., voters] in each state shall have the qualifications requisite for electors of the most numerous branch of the state legislature." (When the principle of direct popular election was extended to senators, this provision was also applied to them; Amendment XVII, Section 1.) Moreover, the Constitution leaves it to each state to "appoint, in such manner as the legislature thereof may direct," the state's delegation to the Electoral College that chooses the President and Vice President (Article II, Section 1).

On the other hand, the Constitution forbids the federal government and the states to deny or abridge, "on account of race, color, or previous condition of servitude" (Amendment XV) or "on account of sex" (Amendment XIX), the right of citizens to vote, and it confers on Congress the power to enforce these articles "by appropriate legislation." In addition, it authorizes Congress to alter state regulations, or to make its own, on "the Times, Places and Manner of holding Elections for Senators and Representatives" (Article I, Section 4). But Congress for many years took only limited action on elections, leaving battles over the suffrage to the courts and the state governments. See V. O. Key, Jr., *Politics, Parties, and Pressure Groups,* 4th ed. (New York: Crowell, 1958), Chapter XXII.

Then, in 1957 and 1960, under the foregoing constitutional provisions and under court interpretations of the "equal protection of the laws" clause of the Fourteenth Amendment, Congress enacted two civil rights acts aimed primarily at protecting the voting rights of Negroes. So the federal government is more involved than ever before in determining eligibility to vote. Still, the states play a much greater role by far; federal action remains supervisory and relatively limited compared to the range of powers exercised by the states in this sphere.

[5] Republican members of Congress from areas that are essentially Republican one-party strongholds (frequently of a rural character) enjoy the same advantage, and reap the same benefits, when their party is in the majority. And the consequences for urban-oriented, socially innovative proposals are often much the same as when their Democratic counterparts occupy key legislative posts.

A Family of Governments

tions have permitted the Republicans to develop a strategy for defeating Democratically sponsored measures of other kinds, such as housing and aid to education, by introducing civil rights provisions into these bills and thus dividing the Democrats. In exactly what ways the pattern of federal legislation would be different had there been no disfranchisement of Negroes is hard to say, but it certainly would have been altered in *some* significant respects. What happens in Congress, then, is as much an outcome of state and local politics as of politics in Washington itself.

In all the United States, only two elected officials represent a territorial constituency larger than a state—the President and Vice President. Yet even they do not represent a single national constituency, for they are chosen by the Electoral College rather than by direct popular vote, and the presidential and vice-presidential electors are elected by states. To be sure, the Electoral College no longer exerts the independent choice that its designers originally intended; with the growth of parties, the electors came automatically to cast their ballots for the candidates of their respective parties except in the rarest instances. Nevertheless, the fact that *all* the electors of the party that wins in any state are elected regardless of the size of the party's majority or plurality means that candidates for the nation's highest offices think in terms of capturing strategic states rather than simply of obtaining a national majority. And no President intent on his own re-election, or eager to improve the chances of victory of a successor from his own party, can afford to ignore the requests and suggestions of the state organizations of his own party with regard to governmental policy and personnel. That is, the mode of election of the President and Vice President compels these officers to bear state politics in mind.

As a matter of fact, it is this very circumstance that probably lies behind some of the proposals for dividing the Electoral College votes of each state in proportion to the popular votes in each state.[6] The present arrangement induces presidential candidates to pay special attention to the most populous states (i.e., the large, industrial, urban states) because they have the largest blocs of electors. But in these states party competition also is fairly close. If Electoral-College delegations were divided according to popular vote, then these states could never deliver much more than half of any delegation to either party. The *one*-party states, on the other hand, though smaller in population, could deliver virtually *all* their votes to the candidate of the party that dominates each of them. The result, of course, would be to increase the influence of the one-party states' politicians in presidential politics, and to reduce the weight of the two-party states. Thus do state political considerations, and considerations of rural as against urban influence, make themselves felt at the federal level.

These considerations are still more evident in the methods of nominating candidates for the Presidency and Vice Presidency. As everyone knows, the presidential nominating conventions are assemblies of delega-

6 For a discussion of various proposals for altering the operation of the Electoral College system see Lucius J. Wilmerding, Jr., *The Electoral College* (New Brunswick, N.J.: Rutgers University Press, 1958).

A Family of Governments

tions from the states that function under rules adopted by each of the parties. The rules of each party differ, but they do have several common characteristics, among which is the practice of relating the size of the delegation from each state to the size of its total representation in Congress and to the strength shown by the party in each state in prior elections. The composition of each delegation, in turn, is determined by state party rules and state election laws, and these rules and laws ordinarily reflect settlements among the local factions within each party and between the parties in each state. A man who seeks the presidential nomination of his party must thus come to terms with the most powerful of the state delegations and with the most powerful local elements in each delegation (which obviously gives great strength to the delegations from the largest states and from the one-party states in which the party in question is dominant). If a man enters the arena with no special advance awareness of the key role that state and local politics play in the nomination and election of a President, he will certainly have acquired that awareness before he emerges from the contest, whether or not he wins it.

That awareness is likely to be intensified if he is elected President. In the first place, he will have made many commitments in regard both to policy appointments during the course of his campaign, commitments which he will be unable to ignore without risking a split in his own party. In the second place, he will have to work to build a working congressional majority out of the variety of state and local interests represented in Congress. In the third place, he will often find that many of his own appointees, since they owe their offices less to him personally than to the coalitions of state and local factions that put their names forward, are not so much subordinates to be directed as colleagues to be bargained with, and that appointments to lesser federal offices requiring senatorial confirmation (such as federal district judgeships) must be acceptable to the senators of the states involved, because the practice of senatorial courtesy confers on senators what amounts to an absolute veto in such cases.

Even our two truly national elective officials, then, the President and the Vice President, never escape the forces of state and local politics. Even these offices must be interpreted in terms of forces at play within the states and within the political subdivisions of the states.

STATES, LOCALITIES, AND CONSTITUTIONAL CHANGE

Governments evolve in many ways, ranging from explicit modifications of organic laws, through reinterpretation of existing language, to changes in practice that are effected without formal or explicit decision. It would not be difficult to find examples of all these types of change in the evolution of the Constitution of the United States. We will not digress, however, to pursue this investigation here; the point to be made is that state and local politics enter into the process of change no matter what the method of change happens to be.

This fact is most evident in the procedures by which the Constitution is amended. No amendment may be adopted without the assent of at least three-fourths of all the states (acting through their legislatures or through statewide conventions convened for the purpose, as the proposed amend-

6

A Family of Governments

ment may provide). The most obvious and dramatic effect of this provision is to guarantee the states against attenuation of their powers by amendment unless there is overwhelming sentiment for such measures throughout the country. Beyond this consideration, however, many proposals doubtless never get past the initial stages of the amendment procedure, because it is apparent they would stand no chance of winning approval in the required number of states. Furthermore, proposed constitutional amendments are formulated and drafted with a view to satisfying all whose support is needed for adoption. In other words, amendments are filtered through a mesh of state and local politics in the course of ratification.

And in the course of initiation, as well. States may initiate proposed amendments if two-thirds of them join in the action, but they have never successfully employed this method.[7] Rather, their principal leverage has been exerted in Congress, where a two-thirds majority in each house is required for the formal proposal of an amendment. Thus, any collection of 34 senators can prevent a measure from even being proposed to the states for ratification. Political opposition in important areas of 17 states, then, may block such action.

What is more, even the adoption of amendments does not assure that they will promptly cause sweeping changes. The Fourteenth and Fifteenth Amendments, for example, did not substantially alter the position or the political effectiveness of Negroes for several generations, and the Eighteenth in all probability did not materially reduce drinking. By lack of co-operation, evasive legislation, biased administrative action, extended litigation, and overt opposition and resistance, states and their subdivisions may succeed in blunting, long delaying, and perhaps even nullifying the effects of provisions of the Constitution to which they strongly object.

In sum, the form, substance, and fate of constitutional amendments are determined to a considerable extent by state and local political factors. And this conclusion about the formal amending process applies still more emphatically to the less formal modes of constitutional evolution.

Consider, for instance, the federal courts in their roles as interpreters (though by no means the sole interpreters) of the Constitution. Regional considerations stand among the important premises of choice for Supreme

[7] Article V of the Constitution of the United States provides two ways to initiate amendments (by two-thirds vote of both houses of Congress, or by a national convention called by Congress on application by the legislatures of two-thirds of the states) and two ways to ratify them (by the legislatures in three-fourths of the states, or by state conventions in three-fourths of the states). All adopted amendments were initiated by the first method of proposal, and all but one were ratified by the first method of approval.

In 1957 the Tennessee General Assembly became the thirty-third state legislative body to memorialize Congress for an amendment to the Constitution limiting federal income-tax rates, thus seemingly meeting the two-thirds requirement (there being 49 states at the time). See Frank E. Packard, "Constitutional Law: The States and the Amending Process," *American Bar Association Journal*, Vol. 45, No. 2 (February, 1959), pp. 161 ff. Congress, however, did not call a constitutional convention, nor did it propose the amendment on its own. Whether it could have been compelled to call a convention remains a moot point, for defects in the applications of several of the states may have invalidated their applications and relieved Congress in this instance of any obligation to act. See Bernard Fensterwald, Jr., "Constitutional Law: The States and the Amending Process—A Reply," *American Bar Association Journal*, Vol. 46, No. 7 (July, 1960), pp. 717 ff.

7

Court appointments. For the lower federal courts, the claims of the state politicians are even more insistent, and, partly because of the senatorial courtesy mentioned earlier, even more effective. Many federal judges thus owe their positions to political forces in their home areas. This is not to say that federal courts reach their decisions by conferring with state political leaders, or that judges are obligated solely to state political units for their elevation to the bench. On the contrary, these factors probably are generally outweighed by juridical traditions, personal preferences, professional values, and the temper of the times, especially since the life tenure and salary protections conferred by the Constitution and by law grant federal judges a substantial measure of immunity to the ordinary pressures of political life. Nevertheless, the fact that judges ascend to their positions via the ladder of state and local politics probably tends to screen out many aspirants to whom such politics is uncongenial, and to provide a judiciary whose decisions reflect at least in some degree the prevailing beliefs and standards of the system from which they spring.[8] In interpreting the Constitution and statutes, as in formulating and enforcing them, states and localities are not without influence, both deliberate and inadvertent. And this influence is further magnified by the frankly partisan selection of United States Attorneys and their assistants, whose discretion in the selection of cases to prosecute, compromise, or drop in many respects gives content to the law; even more than judges, these officers (who may be dismissed from their posts) are beholden for their appointments to their fellow politicians in their respective areas.

A judicial decision is seldom the last word in interpreting the Constitution and statutes.[9] For example, when the Supreme Court decided a case brought without Georgia's consent by citizens of South Carolina against the State of Georgia, the reaction among the state governments and their delegations in Congress was so sharp that the Eleventh Amendment to the Constitution, denying the Supreme Court jurisdiction in such cases, was promptly proposed and ratified.[10] Again, when the Court ruled invalid certain types of state legislation governing minimum prices to be charged by retailers, the states affected and their members of Congress quickly secured passage by Congress of an act validating such legislation.[11] And when a coalition of some of those states off whose shores lie vast reservoirs of undersea oil was unable to persuade the Supreme Court that the Constitution allocated authority over these resources to those states, the representatives and senators from the interested states

[8] Cf., David B. Truman, *The Governmental Process* (New York: Knopf, 1951), pp. 489–490; Jack W. Peltason, *Federal Courts in the Political Process* (New York: Random House, 1955), Chapter IV; John R. Schmidhauser, *The Supreme Court: Its Politics, Personalities, and Procedures* (New York: Holt, Rinehart and Winston, 1960), Parts I and II; Walter F. Murphy and C. Herman Pritchett, *Courts, Judges, and Politics* (New York: Random House, 1961), pp. 67–96.

[9] For ways in which judicial decisions are circumvented or reversed, see Jack W. Peltason, *Federal Courts in the Judicial Process* (Garden City, N.Y.: Doubleday, 1955), pp. 58–62; and Henry J. Abraham, *Courts and Judges* (New York: Oxford University Press, 1959), pp. 37–38.

[10] The case was Chisholm v. Georgia, 2 Dallas 419 (1793). The Eleventh Amendment was proposed by Congress in 1794, declared ratified in 1798.

[11] The case was Schwegmann Bros. v. Calvert Distillers Corp., 341 U.S. 956 (1951). The response was the McGuire Act, 66 *Stat.* 632 (1952).

A Family of Governments

joined hands and mobilized sufficient support in Congress to secure legislation that substantially modified the Court's decision.[12]

Constitutional shifts also take place as bargains are struck, settlements reached, and compromises negotiated in the ordinary course of political life. Many metropolitan regions—i.e., complexes of core cities, satellite cities, and surrounding suburbs—have begun to manifest dissatisfaction with their inability to win from the legislatures of their respective states the kind of sympathetic attention and support their leaders think they need and deserve.[13] Consequently, they have begun to turn increasingly to the federal government for assistance. Although their representation in Washington is, as noted above, not quite in proportion to the population they contain, their concerted efforts constitute a force to be reckoned with, and their allies among the federal agencies, the senators and governors (whose constituencies, after all, are not confined to rural areas), and their influence with the President have secured a hearing for them. Slowly, but increasingly, the federal government has begun in some matters to deal directly with subdivisions of the state rather than with the state governments themselves, until recently the normal channel. The Constitution of the United States is silent on local government, and the states have therefore been regarded as the creator and guardian of these subdivisions. In all probability, political scientists at the turn of the next century will be astounded at the changes in this pattern, especially since the transformation will most likely be accomplished quite gradually and without explicit changes in the wording or interpretation of the Constitution.

So what the Constitution actually *provides*, what it is construed to *mean*, and what *effects* it actually *has*, depend heavily on the strategies and outlooks of governmental and party officers located in, or with roots in, the states and localities.

[12] In 1947 and 1950 the Supreme Court held that the United States, and not the individual states, had paramount rights in and power over the submerged lands; United States v. California, 332 U.S. 19 (1947); United States v. Louisiana, 339 U.S. 699 (1950); United States v. Texas, 339 U.S. 707 (1950). Efforts to counteract these decisions by legislation failed when President Truman vetoed such bills in 1946 and 1952. But President Eisenhower was more favorably disposed, and the Submerged Lands Act (67 *Stat.* 29) and the Outer Continental Shelf Lands Act (67 *Stat.* 462) became law in 1953. (Litigation over the meaning of the acts has continued for many years, however; the issue may still not be closed.) See Ernest R. Bartley, *The Tidelands Oil Controversy: A Legal and Historical Analysis* (Austin: University of Texas Press, 1953); Lucius J. Barker, "The Offshore Oil Controversy Since 1953," *Wisconsin Law Review*, Vol. 1958, No. 1 (January, 1958), pp. 107 ff.; "The Tidelands Oil Controversy," *De Paul Law Review*, Vol. X, No. 1 (Autumn–Winter, 1960), pp. 116 ff.; "Federalism—Submerged Lands Act—Statutory Interpretation," *University of Cincinnati Law Review*, Vol. 29, No. 4 (Fall, 1960), pp. 510 ff.

[13] See Note 3.
But it should not be assumed that reapportionment would automatically make state legislatures all at once receptive to every urban claim. Other factors—for example, partisan differences, factional fights within parties, urban pressure groups that consider state governments more responsive to their demands than are city governments, and the differences in outlook that tend to develop when statewide rather than purely local considerations are injected into the machinery of decision-making—may also tend to prevent cities from getting everything they want and believe they deserve in their state capitals. In some states quite unequally apportioned, cities may fare as well or better than in states where the disparities are much less pronounced.

9

Since the structure, composition, and procedures of the federal government are so basically affected by state and local politics and politicians, it follows that the substance of federal policies must also be influenced, for how a government is set up and who occupies the seats of power are among the chief determinants of what the government will do and will not do. Our discussion thus far, however, by no means exhausts the list of state and local influences that impinge on national politics. Even without the intricate interlocking of levels of government through the mechanisms we have already mentioned, the states and localities would still have available many methods of impressing themselves on the formation and execution of national policy.

For one thing, like other groups in American society, including administrative agencies and parties as well as private organizations, they lobby.[14] Using whatever channels of access they can, they press their claims and demands on Congress, the President, the federal departments, and bureaus, and the courts. They may work together on common problems, operating through the Council of State Governments, or the American Municipal Association, or the United States Conference of Mayors, or through national associations of specialists, such as the Municipal Finance Officers' Association, the National Association of Attorneys General, and the National Conference of Chief Justices. Often, clusters of state or local governments join hands to advance projects and programs of regional concern, such as disposition of the waters of the Colorado River, control of the tidelands' oil resources, or the coinage of silver. Sometimes, states and localities will compete vigorously among themselves for such things as changes in railroad rate structure that might improve their economic position, larger shares of federal expenditures, and even for location of federal installations and branch offices within their boundaries. The methods of exerting pressure extend all the way from personal, friendly, informal contacts to formal appearances before official federal bodies, and to modern public relations techniques. Where appropriate, influence is exercised through the political parties, particularly when individual state and local party organizations have succeeded in communicating a sense of their special importance to influential figures on the national political scene. In short, in a thousand different ways, on all kinds of issues, state and local government officers participate in federal decision-making as lobbyists. We will have more to say about this topic later.

Another way in which state and local governments influence federal policies is by example. Thus, a great deal of the economic regulation now performed by the federal government was pioneered by one or more states. Supervision and control of railroad and utility rates, establishment of maximum hours and minimum wages for workers, adoption of standards

[14] The right "to petition the Government for a redress of grievances" is one of those protected by the First Amendment to the Constitution of the United States, at least as far as private citizens and groups are concerned. In this volume the term "lobby" is used in this general sense, and not as a disparagement, although it must be recognized that some forms of influence have been banned by statute and others may be regarded as questionable in a democratic society whether prohibited or not.

A Family of Governments

for the manufacture and sale of foods and drugs, and regulation of various kinds of business practices are among the kinds of governmental program for which the states showed the way. Similarly, some of our national welfare programs were enacted by the federal government only after a few states had created an appropriate climate of opinion for them by demonstrating their feasibility and desirability. It was at the state level that the earliest public insurance of bank deposits was attempted. Today a number of states have laws prohibiting racial and religious discrimination in employment, education, and places of public accommodation, and New York City has a local law extending this principle to the rental of apartments in privately owned buildings; it is possible that these laws, which, curiously enough, followed limited experimentation in this field by the federal government during World War II, now presage the institution of similar prohibitions on a national scale by the federal government. In most cases, when a state or local government breaks new ground, it apparently does so with its own population and their problems in mind, but chances are good that it also is trying to stimulate national action in this area. At any rate, whether inadvertently or deliberately, states and localities occasionally find initially the paths that Washington subsequently follows.

A third way they influence national policy we already have suggested in another connection, but merits explicit mention: state and local politics is the training ground for national politicians, and most of them learn the objectives, rules, and techniques of politics at these levels before they pass to the national scene. Naturally, there are a few outstanding exceptions to this generalization, particularly the military heroes who have risen to the Presidency. In the main, however, it is a rare national political leader who has not been introduced to politics and the ways of politicians by his state and local experience.

The best way to grasp the significance of this process is to compare it with the way other organizations recruit, train, and advance personnel to the highest positions they can offer. Almost invariably, they rely on service in some lower ranks to prepare men for higher responsibilities, to indoctrinate them with the values of the system, and to provide clues to their ability and personal qualities. The tighter the organization, the more systematic its methods and the greater its success in securing personal identification with the system and in implanting in persons who rise to the top the predisposition to behave in an organizationally sanctioned manner. Big corporations, the military, the Church, and the most widely respected of our civilian public agencies (such as the FBI and the Forest Service), to offer just a few illustrations, all utilize these devices. Similarly, our political system depends on prior experience to weed out aberrants, identify the qualified (which here means those having required political as well as managerial skills), and prepare the successors to present officeholders. For reasons to be discussed presently, political training is far less systematic and far less premeditated than the training in bureaucratic organizations, and therefore does not produce such uniform alumni; this condition yields great benefits but also inflicts some costs. Nevertheless, despite lack of conscious design and rigorous central administration in this training, those persons who come through it do bring with them a respect for the institutions and practices of our governmental machinery that permits an unusually diverse population to govern itself in a reasonably orderly fashion. Above all, such experience tends to generate a tolerance for negotiation and compromise, which inhibits extreme departures from existing programs and policies. This, then, is another reason for regarding state and local government and politics as a major factor in governing the nation; state and local politics set the limits within which the nation is governed.

OUR DECENTRALIZED SYSTEM

In structure, composition, and operation, our national government in all its significant features thus reflects the state and local base on which it rests. Congress, the President, the courts, the Constitution itself, and the very policies the federal government pursues all are shaped by the governments and politics of the states and localities.

Nor do the political parties in this country offset, as they often do in other countries, the fragmentation of governmental structure. On the contrary, the importance of state and local influences in Washington is intensified rather than counterbalanced by the highly decentralized character of our major political parties.

States, Localities, and American Political Parties

WHAT IS CENTRALIZATION?

No one has yet devised a method of measuring organizational centralization, so it is mostly by means of intuitive application of rough clues that we form our impressions about this trait of organizations.

Possibly the chief single index of centralization is the degree to which subordinates in an organization are subjected to central directives that spell out the work they are to do, the way in which it is to be done, and the standards of speed and cost and quality the final products or services must meet. If the top leadership prescribes these instructions in detail, we normally think of an organization as centralized; if the top leadership establishes only a few guidelines and leaves the bulk of such direction to the personnel in the field units, an organization is usually regarded as decentralized.

A second criterion is selection, advancement, and disciplining of the membership, and especially of the lower-ranking leaders, of the organization. The organization is considered centralized when the top leadership has full control over the appointment and removal of subordinates, of the conditions governing the appointing and removal power delegated to subordinates, and when in disciplinary proceedings there is at least a channel of appeal to the highest levels. Organizations are considered decentralized when persons who occupy the formal positions of leadership are seriously restricted in these respects, and when, as a consequence, nominal subordinates owe the leaders little in the way of gratitude and are relatively immune to leadership sanctions.

Third, organizations having central treasuries in which all revenues are deposited, and from which disbursements may be made only on specific authorization of the top leadership, are referred to as centralized. When parts of an organization have their own sources of revenue, their own credit, and expend their resources as they see fit, the organization is called decentralized.

Fourth, decentralized organizations generally have very little machinery for keeping the top leadership apprised of what their subordinates are actually doing. Highly centralized organizations are usually marked by extensive systems of reporting, inspection, and central record-keeping.

Fifth, the field personnel of centralized organizations usually refer questions to their superiors for review and prior clearance; in decentralized organizations, such referral and consultation are much rarer.

Sixth, centralized organizations often develop ways of building loyalty to the top leadership vis-à-vis identification with the component units; rotation of personnel from unit to unit and centrally planned courses for indoctrination of personnel are such devices. In decentralized organizations such practices often are not followed at all, and, when they are, tend to stress individual ties with the component units rather than with the parent association.

This list is far from exhaustive, but it will serve the immediate purpose. Remember that the terms "centralized" and "decentralized" are not used here as mutually exclusive categories, but as polar positions on a continuum from the most centralized to the most decentralized organizations, a continuum on which any organization may be located and compared with any other organization according to their respective composite scores on all the suggested measures on the list. Bear in mind also that the formal documents of an organization do not necessarily portray its nature accurately. In practice, a situation that appears tightly controlled by the terms of an organization's charter and working manuals will often present the leaders with far fewer command opportunities and far less leverage on their subordinates than the formal documents indicate (as any public chief executive in the United States quickly learns, to his dismay). An apparently loosely knit association, on the other hand, may in fact be rigorously directed from a central control point (as any student of the Soviet Union is aware). Within these limits, the indices of centralization permit us to assess the degree of unity our parties possess, and from this assessment to evaluate the capabilities of the parties to furnish a contrary, a centripetal, or coordinate influence that balances the prominent roles of the states and localities in the national government.

THE REMARKABLE DECENTRALIZATION OF OUR PARTIES

By these criteria (and, indeed, perhaps by any other the human mind can contrive), American political parties must be judged so decentralized that they barely qualify as national organizations at all.

The overwhelming bulk of the regulations governing party organization and operation is contained in state legislation enacted by each state individually (primarily representing compromises, bargains, and agreements among the many factions and local groups within the major parties) and in rules adopted under the provisions of the state election laws by state and county committees of each party. Federal statutes deal comparatively briefly with the election of federal officers (President, Vice President, and members of Congress); they do not govern the parties. The national conventions and committees of the parties issue rules relating

13

only to the choice of presidential and vice-presidential candidates and to national platforms. They do not command the state and local units except to the extent that they set the standards for allocating votes at the conventions and decide who is to be seated when competing delegations from individual states claim seats. Beyond this consideration, the directives under which the work of the parties is performed are formulated, promulgated, and enforced entirely at the state and local level.

By the same token, the national leaders of the parties have little to say about who will occupy positions in the state and local units of the parties (or, for that matter, what positions will be established, or even *how* they will be filled). To be sure, a President or a national chairman or both may lend all the support they can muster to one faction or another in a particular state or locality on occasion, and their prestige and the federal patronage they can award or withhold endows them with considerable influence. Nevertheless, even such high-ranking party leaders have been successfully defied by state and local party cliques on occasion, even with regard to the nomination of candidates for Congress, let alone with regard to more obscure positions on party committees or other party posts. The rank-and-file membership and the state and local leadership are all controlled at the state and local levels. The national high command of the major parties more closely resembles the high command of United Nations forces made up of volunteered contingents from various countries than it does the leadership of a national army.

The same is true in connection with party finances. By and large, each unit of a party organization finances its own campaigns. The national committees raise funds for presidential elections, the state committees finance statewide campaigns, and local units or leaders finance contests for lesser state offices or for local offices. Indeed, the national committees depend partly for money on local fund-raisers, so efforts are sometimes made locally to avoid soliciting separately the same donors for different offices in the same election year. Local fund-raisers, however, generally retain a substantial portion of their receipts (to run the campaign in their own areas, or to hold in reserve for other years) as payment for their services. (This practice explains why candidates for chief executive at any level are apt to set up their own fund-raising machinery, over and above the party's regular machinery. This fund assures them that they will have money for appeals through the mass media, and that *all* the money will not be spent by party regulars in contacting voters personally or on candidates for lesser offices.) In a general way, candidates for statewide offices follow the same procedure. Candidates for the minor state elective positions and local offices must bear a heavy share of the financial burden themselves. Consequently the individual units of the party are virtually independent of each other fiscally, and if a higher echelon of the party occasionally puts some of its own money into a campaign for a lower office in which the higher party leaders happen to be especially interested, this move is counterbalanced both by funds raised locally to support candidates for higher offices and by the sums local party units transmit to the higher levels for more extensive campaigning. Not only do state and local party units have resources of their own, not only are they quite able to survive and even flourish with no appropriations or financial support from the higher levels, not only do they independently make their own decisions about the best way to employ their resources, but they may even retaliate against higher party leaders who try to employ financial sanctions against them by the way they conduct and operate the party fund-raising in their areas and the vigor with which they work for party candidates for higher office. If he who pays the piper calls the tune, then state and local components of the major parties dance to their own music.

And so it goes with the other measures of centralization. State and local units of the parties do not report to the national organizations or leaders; they are not inspected by the central leadership, nor does the central leadership perform any regular record-keeping or other staff services for the nominally subordinate elements of the organizations. The subordinates almost never refer matters to higher headquarters for decision, and there is certainly no formal requirement anywhere obliging them ever to do so. Now and then, informally, they may consult with the higher echelons about the "acceptability" of one of their candidates, but even this practice is rare, a courtesy or a tactical maneuver rather than a necessity. As for loyalty to the national leadership of the parties, Republicans and Democrats alike have been plagued by resistance on the part of disappointed state and local politicians, varying in form from failure to work for the national ticket to outright defection to a third party or to the other side. A patriot will defend his country, right or wrong; a soldier may be trained to obey his superiors even when he believes their blunders may cost him his very life; a Communist will follow his leaders though they reverse their positions every other day. But the loyalty of the state and local units to the leaders of an American party is a tenuous thing.

For these reasons Professor V. O. Key of Harvard, one of the country's outstanding experts on parties and politics, concludes that:

> Viewed over the entire nation, the party organization constitutes no disciplined army. It consists of many state and local points of power, each with its own local following and each comparatively independent of external control. Each of the dispersed clusters of party professionals has its own concerns with state and local nominations and election. Each has a base for existence independent of national politics. Each in fact enjoys such independence that more than a tinge of truth colors the observation that there are no national parties, only state and local parties.[15]
>
> The national committee is a gathering of sovereigns (or their emissaries) to negotiate and treat with each other rather than a staff conclave of subordinates of the national chairman.[16]

Under the circumstances, it is quite remarkable that the parties manage to achieve as much harmony and unity as they do during presidential campaigns.

THE CAUSES OF PARTY DECENTRALIZATION

That the parties are decentralized is hardly surprising. In volume, and perhaps even in importance, the targets and rewards of political action are probably greater at the state and local level than at the national level.

Parties, for example, tend to organize themselves around their pri-

[15] Key, *op. cit.*, p. 361.
[16] *Ibid.*, p. 363.

15

A Family of Governments

mary objectives: elective offices. There are about 100,000 units of local government in the country, if we include not only cities, counties, and towns and townships, but school districts (constituting about half the total) and special districts (of which there are over 14,000, handling such functions as fire protection, sewerage, soil conservation, sanitation, and drainage).[17] Most of these units are headed by elected officers or boards, or both. It is not very surprising, therefore, to discover that the total number of elective local officials exceeds 514,000. In addition, there are in the neighborhood of 12,000 to 15,000 elective state officials. A great many of these half million positions, it is true, are not ordinarily sought actively and may even be filled by reluctant incumbents who accept office only because they consider it a civic duty to do so. Even so, the total number aggressively sought by candidates remains high. If half, or as many as two-thirds, of the elective offices in the country were discounted as having little significance, that still would leave over 170,000 to consider.[18]

As we have already mentioned, except for the Presidency and the Vice Presidency, no elected official in the United States has a constituency larger than a state, and most have districts smaller than that. In other words, the overwhelming majority of the offices parties are organized to capture are found at the state and local level. Even if there were no other factors to consider, this fact might be sufficient to account for party decentralization in this country.

There are additional reasons, however. If patronage is considered one of the factors holding party units together, then the fact that there are more appointive offices at the state and local level (all governments taken together) than at the federal level would tend to reinforce the localizing tendencies. The total number of civilian employees of all governments in the United States is over 9 million. Fewer than 2½ million of these are federal; the other 6½ million are state and local (almost 5 million being local only).[19]

Moreover, the merit system is much more fully developed in the federal government than in most state and local governments. Between 85 and 90 per cent of all federal employees are covered by some kind of merit system; fewer than one-half of all the states have merit systems worthy of the name, and most localities do without them. To be sure, most of our 2

[17] See Table 1.

[18] These figures are taken from U.S. Bureau of the Census, *1957 Census of Governments*, Vol. I, No. 4, *Elective Offices of State and Local Governments* (Washington, D.C.: U.S. Government Printing Office, 1958). The following table is on p. 4:

ELECTIVE LOCAL OFFICIALS, by Type of Government and Pay Status, 1957

Type of Government	Total	Paid, Full-time	Paid, Part-time	Unpaid
Number (in thousands):				
All local governments	514.2	68.2	215.7	230.3
Counties	64.2	34.1	23.1	7.0
Municipalities	117.7	10.6	75.6	31.5
Townships	108.0	6.5	77.1	24.4
School districts	188.8	13.9	28.4	146.6
Special districts	35.5	3.1	11.6	20.9

[19] See Tables 13 and 14 and the sources cited therein.

A Family of Governments

million school teachers enjoy some form of protection, and most of our large cities and a substantial proportion of our other cities are covered, so not every state and local government job is filled on a patronage basis. Nevertheless, taking all things into account, the figure for patronage appointments available to the parties at the state and local level must exceed by many times the figure for the federal government. This feature is one of the elements making for the independence of the state and local units of the parties in their relations with the national party leaders. What is more, given all the factors making for decentralization, such federal patronage as still exists is also dispensed through state and local party leaders, for this is one of the ways of winning them over and holding them for national campaigns and of assembling congressional majorities. So appointments tend to have the same effect on the political system as elections; they promote decentralization.

Another form of reward that helps hold party units together is dispensation of special benefits to loyal party workers. Governments, after all, buy a great deal, from electric light bulbs to buildings, from expert advice to insurance. They raise most of their money by taxation. They regulate virtually every kind of business activity. They perform all sorts of services at community expense that might otherwise have to be purchased at individual expense. If a party can obtain for its workers a share of public expenditures these people might not get, if it can secure a favorable ruling or assessment reducing the taxes they have to pay, if it can assure them of licenses they might otherwise have trouble procuring, if it can protect them against rigorous enforcement of regulatory statutes, it can normally keep them working actively in its interests. Sometimes, of course, the favors are very large. Surprisingly often, they are quite minor and almost trivial; a fixed traffic ticket, a stall in a public market, or an intervention on behalf of an individual in slight trouble with the law or with an administrative agency, is frequently the medium of exchange.

Historically, the state and local governments combined spent more, taxed more, regulated more, and served more than the federal government. They no longer spend and tax more, over-all. But they continue to touch the citizen in many more ways than the federal government, and their volume of revenues and expenditures remains vast in the aggregate. Indeed, the scope and depth of state and local governmental activities have grown more rapidly since the end of World War II than have the activities of the federal government. We will have more to say about this trend later. What is relevant here is that the states and localities had more of the special benefits to distribute, which influenced the course of party development, and they still have at their disposal great reserves that can sustain them regardless of what the national party leaders do. This factor adds to the forces that keep state and local party units highly independent and thus decentralize party structure. As a result, national party leaders work through their colleagues at state and local levels in dispensing such special benefits as they can obtain (in spite of stringent federal controls) in order to win local loyalty and support, so even the potentially unifying consequences of favors granted at the national level are dissipated.

Elective office, patronage, and special advantage are by no means the only bonds that hold party organizations together. People work for

17

parties for many reasons, and not all of them are pecuniary. Some do it simply for the fun and excitement, some as an escape from loneliness, some out of a sense of personal friendship for candidates or party leaders, some in the hopes of gaining prestige by associating with public figures, some because they hope to further specific programs or policies to which the party of their choice is committed. Yet these motives and goals also are most easily satisfied at the state and local levels. For at these levels personal contacts are made, personal ties established. At these levels most of our federal officers as well as our governors, mayors, and other officials are nominated and chosen. This is where the work is to be done; campaigns, it must be remembered, are won in the field, not in headquarters. Policy issues of major significance are decided here as well as in Washington, and, as mentioned earlier, even national policies are strongly influenced by states and localities. If America's major parties should one day become frankly ideological, like most European parties, the resulting bodies of ideological doctrine might provide a centralizing tendency that is now absent. But the fate of most ideological parties in this country indicates how improbable is this possibility. The major parties manifest a remarkable capacity to absorb the main planks in the platforms of the ideological associations and thus to rob the third parties of a great deal of their appeal by incorporating those programs into their own eclectic sets of objectives. Anyway, ideological parties themselves must win victories at the state and local level in order to make themselves effective nationally for any extended interval. That is to say, given the governmental arrangements now in effect, and the party arrangements these have engendered, the center of gravity of the party organizations can be expected to remain closer to the base of each party hierarchy than to the apex. The forces in the system tend to sustain this pattern.

This state of affairs alarms many students of American government.[20] In the first place, they believe the lack of cohesion in the parties makes it difficult for either major party, when in power in Washington, to formulate, enact, and enforce a coherent program, with the result that voters have no clear idea of what they are voting for, and no clear standards by which to hold the parties responsible. Consequently, reason the critics, an essential element of democratic government is seriously weakened. In the second place, the present lack of cohesion "poses grave problems of domestic and foreign policy in an era when it is no longer safe for the nation to deal piecemeal with issues that can be disposed of only on the basis of coherent programs."[21] The Committee on Political Parties of the American Political Science Association in 1950 therefore urged a number of measures designed to strengthen national leadership of the parties.[22] This book is not the place to go into these recommendations in detail; suffice it to note, however, that the dynamics of the system, and its defenders, have thus far resisted any pronounced progress in the directions recommended by the committee. Unquestionably there is a great deal

[20] See, e.g., E. E. Schattschneider, *Party Government* (New York: Rinehart, 1942); and American Political Science Association, "Toward a More Responsible Two-Party System: A Report of the Committee on Political Parties," *The American Political Science Review*, Vol. XLIV, No. 3, Part 2 (Supplement), September, 1950.
[21] American Political Science Association, *op. cit.*, p. v.
[22] *Ibid.*, Part 2.

A Family of Governments

that is persuasive in the Committee's arguments when the United States stands confronted by the kinds of international threats and challenges that face it today. But there is much to be said on the other side, too, and, in any event, it is not easy to see how the parties can be changed if our governmental organization remains the same, or how governmental organization can be changed if our parties are not. Continued debate and agitation may eventually achieve what the committee sought to accomplish; if they do, the changes will be gradual and therefore a long time coming, for everything in the system operates to keep it as it is. Good or bad, party decentralization will not soon disappear.

VARIETIES OF STATE AND LOCAL PARTY ORGANIZATION

Because the state and local units of the parties are almost autonomous, they display many different patterns of organization and operation.[23] Speaking of the states alone, Professor Key observes:

In about only a dozen states do the two major parties compete on a fairly even basis. The remainder of the states diverge in varying degrees from the two-party pattern. The net effect . . . means that, in reality, no party system exists within such states for state purposes. The great functions of parties—the construction of coalitions, the designation of candidates, the engineering of consent, the conduct of the government, and so forth—must be performed in these states in one way or another. But they are carried out by more or less amorphous institutions that are hardly the equivalent of party systems in the ordinary usage of the term. The general balance of power within the state— pro-Republican or pro-Democratic—fixes a framework within which factions, in a most bewildering variety of forms, struggle for supremacy within the state. A description of the ins and outs of all the . . . state political systems would fill a shelf of books. . . .[24]

In addition, the *local* patterns are legion. Not only do the conditions under which local party units function vary immensely, from giant metropolis to rural county and village, but the positions of localities similar in size, structure, composition, and legal status may differ from one another because they are set in different kinds of state political systems. So it is difficult to generalize with assurance. Yet one thing seems clear: evenly balanced competition between the parties is as rare at the local level as it is at the state level. In most places a group or a coalition of groups, usually wearing the Republican or Democratic label, consistently controls local offices; the frequency with which control passes from one party to the other on the national scene is virtually unknown, even in some of our largest cities. To be sure, the pendulum does occasionally swing, and the possibilities of defeat are real enough in some places to keep the dominant party constantly on the defensive. But comparatively long periods elapse before swings occur.

Where nomination by a dominant party is tantamount to election to

[23] Key, *op. cit.*, Chapter 11 and pp. 318–368. For other approaches to the varieties of state and local patterns of party organization, see Fred I. Greenstein, *The American Party System and the American People* (Englewood Cliffs, N.J.: Prentice-Hall, 1963), Chapter V.

[24] Key, *op. cit.*, p. 318.

19

A Family of Governments

public office, battles that would otherwise occur between the parties take place among rival factions within the dominant party. Here and there, two persistent factions appear and produce a very rough approximation, but *only* an approximation, of two-party politics. Generally, though, in the states and in local jurisdictions, government is conducted by congeries of individuals with personal followings. In these circumstances, even to a lesser extent than in the national government, the men in office share no common policy commitments, experience no searching criticisms, have little to bind them to one another. In addition, other participants in politics—pressure groups, bureaucracies, newspapers, and others—are able to exert far more influence than they otherwise would.

This is not to say there are *no* cohesive organizations in *any* states and localities; old-fashioned machines still exist even today, and some reformers, employing policy and program instead of patronage and spoils as the attractions, show signs of organizing their followers in as tightly knit a structure as any ever seen at these levels. Moreover, where party units face real competition from the opposing party, they frequently unite to meet the threat.

On the whole, however, state and local components of the major parties are themselves fragmented and operate in their own areas without frequent serious challenges. This is probably as far as we can go in making general statements about them.

STATE AND LOCAL GOVERNMENTAL VITALITY

So our parties reinforce the fragmentation of our governmental system, and add to the need to understand government and politics at the state and local levels in order to understand what goes on in Washington.

But the states and localities also deserve attention in and of themselves. Despite the critical domestic and international responsibilities of the federal government, state and local governments are active, vigorous, and growing. Their importance in the national government and in the parties rests in the last analysis on their continuing performance of vital public functions.

The Division of Governmental Labor

THE SIZE OF THE GOVERNMENTAL JOB

In these days of massive governmental expenditures—all levels of government together in 1960 spent over $151 billion (including disbursements by utilities, liquor stores, and insurance trusts)[25]—it is difficult to realize that the national government, the states, and all the localities were spending only a little over $1.5 billion dollars annually in the first years of this century.[26]

It is equally difficult to realize, in these days of swollen federal budgets, that the states and localities spent more each year (except for

[25] U.S. Bureau of the Census, *Governmental Finances in 1960* (September 19, 1961), p. 1.
[26] See Table 2.

A Family of Governments

Years	Total, All Governments	Federal		State and Local		
			Both		State	Local
1902	1,578	565	36%	1,013	64%	134	8%	879	56%
1913	3,022	958	32	2,064	68	297	10	1,767	58
1922	8,854	3,636	41	5,218	59	1,031	12	4,187	47
1927	10,590	3,380	32	7,210	68	1,380	13	5,830	55
1932	11,748	3,983	34	7,765	66	1,965	17	5,800	49
1936	15,835	8,191	52	7,644	48	2,223	14	5,421	34
1940	18,125	8,896	49	9,229	51	2,730	15	6,499	36
1946	75,582	64,554	85	11,028	15	3,153	4	7,875	11
1948	50,088	32,404	65	17,684	35	6,186	12	11,498	23
1952	91,291	65,193	71	26,098	29	8,653	10	17,444	19
1956	102,628	65,917	64	36,711	36	12,319	12	24,392	24
1960	128,600	76,724	60	51,876	40	17,945	14	33,931	26

ᵃ "Direct general expenditures" exclude expenditures by utilities, liquor stores, and insurance trusts (such as social security, pension funds, etc.), and all intergovernmental expenditures.

Source: U.S. Bureau of the Census, *Governmental Finances in the United States, 1902 to 1957* (March, 1959), pp. 16–25; and *Governmenal Finances in 1960* (September 19, 1961), p. 19.

years of major war and one or two of the depression years) than the federal government until our involvement in World War II.[27]

But most surprising of all is the fact that the states and localities *still* outspend the federal government by far, if federal expenditures connected with wars—past, present, future; hot and cold—are treated as special. What is more, since the end of World War II, the expenditures of state and local governments have increased more rapidly than the non-war-connected expenditures of the federal government. State and local governments have not lost their places in the American political system, and appear even to be gaining ground.

To simplify the picture, we will omit the expenditures by utilities, liquor stores, and insurance trusts (all of which are self-financing activities for the most part) and transfers of funds between governments, and will concentrate exclusively on the direct general expenditures by each level of government. In 1960 these expenditures came to over $76 billion for the federal government and to almost $52 billion for the state and local governments, making a total of more than $128 billion over-all. The federal figure, however, includes more than $47 billion for national defense and international relations, close to $4 billion for services to veterans, and in excess of $7.5 billion for interest on the national debt, most of which was incurred to pay the costs of war.[28] If we count only $4 billion

[27] *Ibid.*

[28] See Tables 4, 5, 6.
The federal debt climbed from $1.2 billion in 1915 to $25.5 billion in 1919, chiefly as a result of World War I. During World War II it rose from $40.4 billion in 1939 to $269.4 billion in 1946. Before the Korean war it was $252.8 billion (1949); afterwards (1954), it was $271.3 billion. U.S. Bureau of the Census, *Statistical Abstract of the United States, 1961* (82nd ed., Washington, D.C., 1961), p. 389.

21

of the debt service charges as war-connected, which is a very conservative estimate, the sum devoted to war-connected activities and international relations comes to over $55 billion, or 72 per cent of the federal total, leaving only $21 billion for all other functions. By contrast, virtually all the state and local activities had little or nothing to do with war and

Table 3   A COMPARISON OF GOVERNMENTAL INDEBTEDNESS (in millions of dollars)ᵃ
by All Levels of Government in Selected Years

Year	Total, All Governments	Federal	State and Local		
			Both	State	Local
1902	3,285	1,178	2,107	230	1,877
1913	5,607	1,193	4,414	379	4,035
1922	33,072	22,963	10,109	1,131	8,978
1927	33,393	18,512	14,881	1,971	12,910
1932	38,692	19,487	19,205	2,832	16,373
1936	53,253	33,779	19,474	3,413	16,061
1940	63,251	42,968	20,283	3,590	16,693
1946	285,339	269,422	15,917	2,353	13,564
1948	270,948	252,292	18,656	3,676	14,980
1952	289,205	259,105	30,100	6,874	23,226
1956	321,911	272,751	49,161	12,890	36,271
1960	356,286	286,331	69,955	18,543	51,412

ᵃ Utilities' indebtedness included.
Source: U.S. Bureau of the Census, Governmental Finances in the United States, 1902 to 1957 (March, 1959), pp. 16–25; Governmental Finances in 1960 (September 19, 1961), p. 22; Statistical Abstract of the United States, 1961 (82nd ed.; Washington, 1961), p. 389.

represented direct services to the people. Viewed from this angle, the states and localities spent almost two and a half times as much as the federal government on such functions.[29]

In 1948, when the economy had virtually been converted from a wartime to a peacetime footing, and prior to the Korean War and other international crises, the direct general expenditures of the federal government came to about $32 billion, of which at least $21 billion (66 per cent) were war-connected in the sense used above, leaving some $11 billion for all the other functions. State and local governments in the same year spent over $17 billion.[30]

Thus, in the course of 11 years, federal expenditures not connected with war and international relations increased less than twice, whereas state and local expenditures more than tripled. From these figures it would seem that the rise in the federal budget represents not a tendency on the part of the federal government to swallow up the states and their subdivisions, but rather a program for preserving the system in which these governments are able and helped to expand and prosper.[31]

[29] And perhaps even more! See Note a, Table 6.
[30] See Tables 4, 5, 6, and U.S. Bureau of the Census, Government Finances in the United States, 1902 to 1957 (March, 1959), pp. 18, 20.
[31] Over and above the direct expenditures described here, the federal government gave almost $7 billion to the states. The states, however, gave over $9 billion to local governments. So if intergovernmental expenditures are added to direct ex-

A Family of Governments

This relationship is even more dramatically underscored by the figures on governmental borrowing. The federal government came out of World War II with a debt of approximately $270 billion in 1946; state and local indebtedness in the same year was about $16 billion. By 1960 the federal debt had increased by $16 billion, to $286 billion, but the state and local debt had risen $54 billion, to a total of almost $70 billion.[32] Whether borrowing is the best way to finance government operations is beside the point here; arguments can be made on either side of the question. What this does demonstrate clearly, though, is that there has been no atrophy of state and local governments as far as their assumption of the burdens of service is concerned.

As you might expect, even in non-war-connected expenditures, the federal government concentrates on an array of functions different from that of the state and local governments, although all levels are involved in some degree in almost the whole range of governmental activities. The federal government spent more than $7 billion of its $21 billion non-war budget in 1960 on natural resources (including agriculture), another $3.73 billion on postal service, and nearly another $1.5 billion on health and hospitals; these three functions alone thus consumed almost 58 per cent of the direct non-war federal outlays.[34]

In like fashion, a half dozen functions siphoned off 78 per cent of all state and local expenditures. Three of these functions are virtually exclu-

---

penditures, the state and local increases as compared with the federal increases would be even *more* disproportionate than is suggested in the text. But see Note 34.

Remember in reviewing these figures that no allowance has been made for inflation or increase in population. If these factors are taken into account, the increases in expenditure are not quite so extreme as they might seem at first blush, although by *any* standard they are dramatic. Direct general expenditures by all governments per capita, for example, excluding utilities, liquor stores, and trusts, rose from $19.93 in 1902 to $714.54 in 1960. See U.S. Bureau of the Census, *Governmental Finances in the United States, 1902 to 1957* (March, 1959), p. 15; and *Governmental Finances in 1960* (September 19, 1961), p. 19.

[32] See Table 3.

[33] The figures in this section were computed from U.S. Bureau of the Census, *Governmental Finances in 1960* (September 19, 1961), pp. 18, 19. See Table 7.

[34] These figures do not include grants-in-aid and other forms of intergovernmental expenditure. The reason is that all such grants eventually show up as direct expenditures of the ultimate receiving government. Thus if federal grants to the states were counted separately, and state grants (largely federal moneys supplemented by the states' own revenues) to the localities were also counted separately, and then the final expenditures by the localities were counted separately, the same dollars would be counted three times. To avoid this duplication, we have treated only *direct* expenditures by all governments, not payments to other governments.

It should be noted, however, that federal payments to the states (and in small amounts directly to local governments) came to almost seven billion dollars in 1960 (Tables 10, 16, 17). This would make the total outlay of the federal government somewhat higher, and its showing in non-war expenditures somewhat better. It would not, however, invalidate the point, made in the text, that the range of federal non-war expenditures is limited, for 41 per cent of federal aid was for highways and 30 per cent for public welfare. Thus, even *including* intergovernmental expenditures, these two functions plus the three mentioned in the text above absorb some two-thirds of all federal non-war expenditures.

Table 4   DIRECT GENERAL EXPENDITURE (in millions of dollars)
by War-connected and Non-war connected Functions, by Levels of Government, 1960 and 1948

Function	All Governments		Federal		State and Local					
					Both		State		Local	
All functions (1960)	126,600	100%	76,724	100%	51,876	100%	17,945	100%	33,931	100
War-connected	55,265	43	55,153	72	112	0.2	112	0.6	—ᵃ	—
Non-war-connected	73,335	57	21,571	28	51,764	99.8	17,833	99.4	33,931	100
All functions (1948)	50,088	100%	32,404	100%	17,684	100%	6,186	100%	11,499	100
War-connected	21,964	44	21,331	66	633	3	633	10	—ᵃ	—
Non-war-connected	28,049	56	11,073	34	17,051	97	5,553	90	11,499	100

ᵃ Small amounts for civil defense not separated out.
Note: For other notes and for sources, see Table 7.

sively state and local, for federal funds in these areas are not very substantial: the three are education (with 36 per cent of the total, or more than $18 billion), police and fire protection (5 per cent, or over $2.5 billion), and sewers and sanitation (in excess of 3 per cent—i.e., almost $2 billion). The other three functions are not solely state and local, but state and local expenditures far exceed the federal: these three are highways ($9.5 billion, 18 per cent of all state and local budgets), welfare ($4.5 billion, more than 8 per cent), and health and hospitals (a little under $4 billion, or 7 per cent).[35]

To sum up, eight functions absorb between two-thirds and three-quarters of all governmental expenditures not directly traceable to the preparations for, conduct of, or aftermath of war. Two of these functions

Table 5   DIRECT GENERAL EXPENDITURE (in millions of dollars)
by War-connected and Non-war-connected Functions, by Levels of Government, 1960 and 1948

Level of Government	Total All Functions		War-connected Functions		Non-war-connected Functions	
All levels (1960)	128,600	100%	55,265	100%	73,335	100%
Federal	76,724	60	55,153	99.8	21,571	30
State and local	51,876	40	112	0.2	51,764	70
State	17,945	14	112	0.2	17,833	24
Local	33,931	26	—ᵃ	—	33,931	46
All levels (1948)	50,088	100%	21,964	100%	28,049	100%
Federal	32,404	65	21,331	97	11,073	39
State and local	17,684	35	633	3	17,051	61
State	6,186	12	633	3	5,553	20
Local	11,498	23	—ᵃ	—	11,498	41

ᵃ Small amounts for civil defense not separated out.
Note: For other notes and for sources, see Table 7.

[35] State payments to local governments came to more than $9 billion in 1960 (Tables 10, 16, 17). As explained in Footnote 34, these are not included in the figures cited in the text in order to avoid duplicate counting. This means more money passes through the hands of the state governments than is reflected in the direct expenditure figures, and makes the states' role in peaceful expenditures even greater. It does not change the balance among the functions of state and local governments, however, because 86 per cent of all state aid goes for education, highways, and public welfare, which are high on the list of major activities even without grants.

A Family of Governments

Table 6 DIRECT GENERAL EXPENDITURE (in millions of dollars)
by War-connected Functions and by Levels of Government, 1960 and 1948

Function	All Governments	Federal	State and Local		
			Both	State	Local
War-connected (total, 1960)	55,265	55,153	112	112	—
Defense, international relations	47,464	47,464	—	—	—
Veterans[a]	3,801	3,689	112	112	—
Interest on war debt	4,000	4,000	—	—	—
War-connected (total, 1948)	21,964	21,331	633	633	—
Defense, international relations	15,538	15,538	—	—	—
Veterans[a]	3,926	3,293	633	633	—
Interest on war debt	2,500	2,500	—	—	—

[a] Actually, expenditures on veterans are at least $2 billion higher, for some of these expenses are allocated to non-war-connected functions by the Bureau of the Census; see its *Governmental Finances in 1960* (September 19, 1961), p. 20.
Note: For other notes and for sources, see Table 7.

(natural resources and postal services) are essentially federal. The others are mainly state and local, and even federal grants are ultimately disbursed by state and local officials. So these large-scale expenditures and activities that have nothing to do with international tensions point up the continuing vitality of the smaller units of government in the United States.

The same is true of the less costly activities as well. The $7 billion of direct federal expenditure not accounted for above are allocated to a wide variety of agencies and activities, including the Federal Communications Commission, the Securities and Exchange Commission, the Interstate Commerce Commission, the regulation of aviation and airways, the Department of Justice and all its subdivisions, and many others.[36] These are all vital services. At the same time, however, the states and localities are spending some $11 billion, not covered above, on parks and playgrounds, traffic control, motor-vehicle registration and testing of drivers, planning and redevelopment, libraries, supervision and control of public utilities, building inspection, licensing of trades and professions and businesses, regulation of banks and insurance companies, and dozens of other functions.[37] In order words, by any index, the states and their subdivisions are not wasting away. On the contrary, responsibilities of defense apart, they carry a larger share of the burdens of public service than does the federal government. In the United States federalism is not a sham or a vestigial form; it is a flourishing system of politics.

In this connection it is worthwhile to pause and examine briefly the divisions of functions between the states and the local governments. For the localities, contrary to what one might expect, carry far more of the

[36] Similarly, the 29 per cent of federal aid to the states not accounted for by highway and welfare grants is spread much more thinly over a diverse aggregate of activities (Table 10).

[37] The direct expenditures are supplemented by an additional billion dollars of state aid not earmarked for education, highways, and welfare (Table 10).

A Family of Governments

Table 7   GENERAL EXPENDITURE (in millions of dollars)ᵃ, by Non-war connected Functions and by Levels of Government, 1960 and 1948

Functions	All Governments		Federal		Both		State and Local			
							State		Local	
Non-war-connected Totalᵉ (1960)	73,335	100%	21,571	100%	51,764	100%	17,945	100%	33,931	100%
Resources and agriculture	8,414	12	7,225	34	1,189	2	842	5	347	1
Postal service	3,730	5	3,730	17	—	—	—	—	—	—
Health and hospitals	5,245	7	1,450	7	3,790	7	1,896	10	1,899	6
Highways	9,565	13	137	0.6	9,428	18	6,070	34	3,358	10
Public welfare	4,462	6	58	0.3	4,404	9	2,221	12	2,183	6
Education	19,404	27	685ᵈ	3	18,719	36	3,557	20	15,162	45
Police and fire	3,025	4	173	0.8	2,852	6	245	1	2,607	8
Sewers and sanitation	1,727	2	—	—	1,727	3	—	—	1,727	5
Interest, non-war debtᵇ	5,332	7	3,662	17	1,670	3	536	3	1,134	3
General controlᶜ	2,859	4	746	3	2,113	4	654	4	1,459	4
Other	9,572	13	3,705	17	5,872	12	1,924	11	4,055	12
Non-war-connected Totalᵉ (1948)	28,049	100%	11,073	100%	17,051	100%	5,553	100%	11,498	100%
Resources and agriculture	2,223	8	1,727	16	496	3	344	6	152	1
Postal service	1,715	6	1,715	15	—	—	—	—	—	—
Health and hospitals	1,934	7	705	6	1,229	7	663	12	566	5
Highways	3,071	11	35	0.3	3,036	18	1,510	27	1,526	13
Public welfare	2,144	8	45	0.4	2,099	12	962	17	1,137	10
Education	7,721	28	2,342ᵈ	21	5,379	32	1,081	20	4,298	37
Police and fire	1,130	4	80	0.7	1,050	6	65	1	985	9
Sewers and sanitation	670	2	—	—	670	4	—	—	670	6
Interest, non-war debtᵇ	2,222	8	1,823	17	399	2	86	2	313	3
General controlᶜ	1,325	5	445	4	880	5	266	5	614	5
Other	3,894	13	2,156	19	1,813	11	576	10	1,237	11

ᵃ "Direct general expenditures" exclude expenditures by utilities, liquor stores, and insurance trusts (social security, pension funds, etc.), and all intergovernmental expenditures. Thus federal expenditures on highways, welfare, and other federally aided programs show up as very low, because this money is disbursed directly by the states and localities to which it is granted. For intergovernmental expenditures, see Table 10.

ᵇ Estimated. The total interest was divided between war-incurred debt and other debt. The estimate is conservative, since more of the federal debt was incurred in wartime than in peace. See Table 3 and Note 28.

ᶜ Consists of the activities of governmental chief executives and their staffs, legislative bodies, administration of justice, and financial and other general administration.

ᵈIncludes expenditures for the education of veterans.

ᵉTotal percentages may not add up to 100 because of rounding.

Sources: U.S. Bureau of the Census, *Governmental Finances in 1960* (September 19, 1961), pp. 18, 20; *Governmental Finances in the United States, 1902 to 1957* (March, 1959), pp. 16–25; *State Government Finances in 1960* (1961), p. 9.

Table 8 ALL DIRECT GOVERNMENTAL EXPENDITURES (In millions of dollars)
Including Expenditures by Utilities, Liquor Stores, and Insurance Trusts,
by Character, Object, and Levels of Government, 1960

	All Governments	Federal	State and Local Both	State and Local State	State and Local Local
General expenditures[a]	128,600	76,724	51,876	17,945	33,931
Utility expenditures[b]	4,066	—	4,066	—	4,066
Liquor stores expenditures	1,022	—	1,022	907	115
Insurance trust expenditures[c]	17,596	13,565	4,031	3,461	570
Total direct expenditures	$151,288	$90,289	$60,999	$22,313	$38,686

[a] See Table 7 for functional breakdowns.
[b] Water supply, electric power, transit, and gas supply systems.
[c] Unemployment compensation; employee retirement; old age, survivors, and disability insurance; veterans insurance; and railroad retirement make up the principal items in this category.
Source: U.S. Bureau of the Census, Governmental Finances in 1960 (September 19, 1961), pp. 17, 21, 22.

joint load than do the state governments. Of the 52 billion dollars spent directly by state and local governments in 1960 (not including grants-in-aid and other intergovernmental payments), local governments spent $34 billion, the states $18 billion. The bulk of the direct state expenditures were for education, highways, health and hospitals, and welfare. The localities were heavily involved not only in these areas (much more so than the states in the case of education, for which they spent more than $15 billion as against a little over $3.5 billion for the states), but also in police, fire protection, sewerage and sanitation, parks, libraries, air transportation, water terminals, and other services on which the state govern-

Table 9 ALL DIRECT GOVERNMENTAL EXPENDITURES (in millions of dollars)
Including Expenditures by Utilities, Liquor Stores, and Insurance Trusts,
by Character, Object, and Levels of Government, 1960

	All Governments	Federal	State and Local Both	State and Local State	State and Local Local
Current operation	81,654	45,336	36,318	9,694	26,624
Capital outlay	31,946	16,842	15,104	6,607	8,497
Construction	15,832	3,480	12,352	5,509	6,843
Equipment	14,378	13,186	1,192	296	896
Land and structures	1,735	175	1,560	802	758
Assistance and subsidies	10,402	6,884	3,518	2,015	1,503
Interest and debt	9,690	7,662	2,028	536	1,492
Insurance benefits and repayments	17,596	13,565	4,031	3,461	570
Total direct expenditures	$151,288	$90,289	$60,999	$22,313	$38,686
Exhibit: expenditure for personal services	$ 44,768	$20,323[a]	$24,445	$ 6,055	$18,390

[a] Includes $7,423 million for military personnel.
Source: U.S. Bureau of the Census, Governmental Finances in 1960 (September 19, 1961), p. 17.

A Family of Governments

Table 10   INTERGOVERNMENTAL EXPENDITURES (in millions of dollars)[a]
by Functions and Levels of Government, 1960

Functions	State Payments to Local Governments[b]	Federal Payments to	
		States	Local Governments
Total[d]	9,283	6,352	642
Education	5,300	705	245
Highways	1,247	2,905	c
Natural resources	20	127	c
Health and hospitals	176	135	c
Public welfare	1,483	2,070	c
Housing and community development	26	—	226
Air transportation	24	21	35
Social insurance administration	—	325	c
Waste treatment	—	—	40
District of Columbia	—	—	25
Other and combined	1,007	65	71

[a] Eventually, intergovernmental expenditures show up as direct expenditures of the governments that receive the grants, shared taxes, etc. If they were counted both when transferred from one government to another and again when spent by the recipient government, they would be counted twice. Consequently, only direct expenditures are included in figures for total expenditures of all governments (in Tables 4–9, inclusive, and in the text).

[b] There were also payments of $209 million from local governments to states.

[c] Payments, if any, in this category are included under "Other and combined."

[d] Detail may not add up to totals because of rounding.

Source: U.S. Bureau of the Census, Governmental Finances in 1960 (September 19, 1961), pp. 17, 18.

ments spent comparatively little. That is, the decentralization of the American system does not stop at the state level, but reaches the lowest echelons.[38] This point is something to bear in mind when studying national government and politics as well as the government and politics of the states and localities, for it has a profound influence on the things that happen in the national capital and the national parties. In all modern national governments tasks are divided among the central units and the smaller units they encompass. The extent of the devolution of responsibility in the United States is quite unusual, however, especially since the role of the national government in controlling and supervising the local governments is exceptionally limited.

Relations among the Levels of Government

THE PIVOTAL POSITION OF THE STATES

Both the federal government and local governments obtained their powers originally by delegation from the states. In a highly theoretical sense the states possess the means of reclaiming these powers. Since the states can initiate amendments to the Constitution of the United States (by joint action of at least two-thirds of them) and then ratify the amendments, it is not completely impossible for such exceptionally large majorities to modify or even to abolish the Constitution if they wish. Since, moreover, virtually all forms of government within the states are generally treated in

[38] Even the state aid described earlier is disbursed chiefly through local governmental units.

28

A Family of Governments

law as "creatures of the state," subject entirely to the will of their respective state governments (within the limits imposed on the state governments by the people of the states through their state constitutions), the states could conceivably reorganize the structure of local government drastically at any time.

Obviously, revolutionary changes of this character are only very remote possibilities. In the first place, the conditions that persuaded the states to adopt the Constitution in the first instance have intensified rather than abated over time. If it was advisable to establish a central government of broad authority in the eighteenth century, this is an inescapable necessity today. Had the original states found some form of association that would have enabled them to survive until now without a national government, today they certainly would feel compelled to establish some kind of central authority. Even the traditional rivalries and suspicions of the countries of Europe are giving way to the pressures of the times; there has been more progress toward European union in recent decades than for centuries previous. Consequently, the probabilities of the states moving in the opposite direction, even if they could actually mobilize to exercise the options embodied in the Constitution, are negligible.

Similarly, the reasons for delegating to subdivisions of the states those powers they now possess have grown more persuasive with the passage of the years. Admittedly, the isolation of communities in earlier days, which was a major reason for delegation, has been dispelled by modern technology and the growth of population. But the value attached to local independence and self-government, a spirit engendered by the experience and circumstances of the original settlers, has shown a remarkable capacity to endure (sometimes in the form of sentimental attachments to units of government possibly outmoded by the growth of metropolitan regions). Furthermore, locally rendered public services have increased immensely in number and variety in recent years. To the traditional functions of road construction and maintenance, law enforcement and adjudication, and education, the advance of industrialism and scientific knowledge has added many more, such as public health and sanitation, hospitals, modern programs of public welfare and assistance, land-use planning and regulation, public parks and recreation, and others. What began as a matter of choice and convenience has now become an administrative necessity; delegation of governmental responsibility and authority to communities is now virtually unavoidable.

In the second place, once a set of political arrangements has been adopted and set in motion, it quickly generates forces within itself that resist change, and resist especially forcefully those changes that might alter or destroy its major features, or extensively modify relationships among its parts. People develop commitments to a system. Emotional attachments and loyalties spring up. Persons or groups who enjoy advantages are reluctant to risk their favored positions. Many grow uneasy about substituting unknown institutions for familiar and well-understood ones.

So the fact that the states are not categorically prevented from rescinding the powers they have delegated to the federal government and to their own subdivisions does not mean that such a move would be a practical possibility. On the contrary, although one or two cities have at dif- **29** ferent times been temporarily stripped of their powers by so-called ripper legislation enacted for partisan political reasons by their state legislatures,[39] recent trends have all been in the other direction. The bases of both federal and local governments grow firmer, not weaker, with time.

Yet the *evolution* of the American system *has* been profoundly influenced by the doctrine that the states are the source of authority from which all other governments are derived. The other governments have had to justify in the courts every expansion of activity, every new undertaking, not specifically sanctioned in basic documents, and to secure specific authorizing language in many instances. The localities and the federal government have not enjoyed equal success in these struggles; the former have not made nearly the progress achieved by the latter. What the present system of government is, and how it became what it is, can be explained only in the light of legal theory and historical precedent that places the states in the pivotal position.

"IMPLIED POWERS" VERSUS "DILLON'S RULE"

The Constitution of the United States enumerates the powers conferred on the federal government. But under John Marshall the Supreme Court declared that the language of the Constitution was not to be construed literally; rather, the list of powers specifically delegated was to be interpreted as implying the right to take such action as might be required to make the specified powers effective.[40] The Court has not always construed the Constitution as broadly as Marshall did, but while there have been short-range regressions, the long-range trend has consistently been in the same direction: to permit the federal government to enter into new activities and assume new responsibilities *inferred* from the words of our organic law rather than explicitly stated. The doctrine of implied powers is firmly entrenched in constitutional law, and the powers to regulate interstate commerce, to spend money, and to declare and conduct war have been particularly important vehicles for the increase in federal functions.[41]

The powers of local governments, by contrast, have usually been narrowly construed. This function is largely in the hands of the state courts, not the federal courts, because the delegation of powers from states to local units is not a question lying within the jurisdiction of the federal government. To be sure, an action of a local government may be challenged in a federal court by a citizen who believes the action infringes his rights under the Constitution of the United States (usually under the due process or equal protection clauses of the Fourteenth Amendment). But this situation does not involve the *delegation* of state power; it deals only with the right of the citizen against his governments, and what the states themselves may do, they may as a general rule choose to let their

[39] See Charles M. Kneier, *City Government in the United States,* 3rd ed. (New York: Harper, 1957), pp. 50–54, for a discussion of extreme applications of state legislative power over cities. The most notable cases were those of Memphis in 1879 and a number of Pennsylvania cities in 1901, described in Kneier, pp. 52 and 53.

[40] McCulloch v. Maryland, 4 Wheaton 316 (1819).

[41] Cf., Carl B. Swisher, *The Growth of Constitutional Power in the United States* (Chicago: University of Chicago Press, 1946), Chapters IV, IX.

A Family of Governments

subdivisions do. Whether a power delegated to local governments in a state may be so delegated under the state constitution, and whether an action taken by a local government lies within the power delegated, are not federal questions; they are matters decided within each state. Consequently, when we say the powers of local governments have been narrowly construed, we are talking for all practical purposes of the attitude of state courts toward subdivisions of the states. By and large, the attitude has been one of strict construction. A unit of government whose acts are challenged is commonly required to demonstrate fairly explicit statutory or (state) constitutional authorization for what it has done, or its actions may fall.

What we have just said does not mean that state courts never look beyond the specific wording of constitutions and statutes to determine whether a local subdivision has legal justification to take action. Judges are men of reason and good sense, and are no more inclined than anyone else to insist on such rigid applications of the law as to immobilize the machinery of government. However, whereas federal judges tend to conceive of the Constitution of the United States as a highly elastic document containing by implication many federal powers not stated expressly, state judges are prone to decide against local governments unless delegation is quite explicit and unambiguous. Speaking of municipal corporations, the units of local government invested with the broadest range of powers (about which more will be said in our discussion of forms of local government), Judge John F. Dillon, an authority on the subject, summed up the position of the courts in 1911 in these words: "Any fair, reasonable, substantial doubt concerning the existence of power is resolved by the courts against the [municipal] corporation, and the power is denied."[42] Nothing has happened in the intervening decades to require significant revision of Judge Dillon's "rule," and it applies even more emphatically to other forms of local government than to the municipal corporations about which it was formulated. For local governments, strict construction normally obtains.

As a result of these differences between the interpretation of federal powers and the interpretation of local powers, the federal government has been able to expand without repeatedly returning to the states or resorting to the amending process to adjust to changing conditions, but local governments have been compelled to plead their case in their respective state capitals each time they seek additional authority. This situation has made it possible for the state governments to maintain rather tight control over localities, and thus to exercise a pervasive influence on local government and politics. Local governments are entrusted with the performance of many of the most important public functions in the American system, but they are by no means free and independent. (Local units of the political *parties*, however, are quite autonomous, as we mentioned earlier.) In other words, the American system of government may be described as a federal union of unitary states. The full significance of this statement will emerge as the discussion proceeds.

[42] John F. Dillon, *Commentaries on the Law of Municipal Corporations*, 5th ed. (Boston: Little, Brown, 1911), Vol. I, Sec. 237. See also, Charles S. Rhyne, *Municipal Law* (Washington, D.C.: National Institute of Municipal Law Officers, 1957), pp. 70–72.

A Family of Governments

To governmental officials and politicians in the cities, this state of affairs became increasingly humiliating and, even more important, incapacitating as they tried to come to grips with the problems of rapidly growing urban areas. Rural control of the state legislatures coupled with partisan differences between state governments and city governments aggravated the tensions. After the Civil War, therefore, urban interests began to press for power to frame and adopt and amend their own charters, and for explicit grants of authority over local affairs. To this bundle of proposed reforms, the term "home rule" was applied. The success of the movement has been checkered; about half the states have adopted some provisions of this character, most of them in the form of amendments to the state constitutions, some in the form of ordinary legislation. The measures are by no means uniform; "home rule" has become a slogan of variable content. The common core of the measures is the attempt to reduce the extent of state surveillance and intervention in city government, and to increase the autonomy of the municipalities. In a broad sense, although the objective is never phrased in just these terms, "home rule" is an effort to soften or reverse "Dillon's rule."

In the main, the attempt has fallen far short of the hopes of its advocates. Not even the most ardent supporters of home-rule amendments and legislation ever suggested that the states should relinquish *all* authority over cities. The goal was to establish local control over local affairs, leaving undisturbed the state powers over matters of general concern to the people of the entire state. Drawing the line between what is of local concern and what is of state concern, however, proved to be far more difficult than was originally anticipated. To the courts fell the task of making the determination. Their decisions are not easily characterized in a few words, but they display a tendency to find a great deal of what goes on in cities to be of general interest to the state and therefore subject to state regulations, despite the home-rule provisions. Some significant increases in local independence have been registered; nonetheless, the total picture remains much as it was. Bent but not broken, "Dillon's rule" still prevails.

Relations among the levels of government thus fall into no simple, symmetrical pattern. They are more like a tangled web of rubber bands—intricate, elastic, capable of accommodating all sorts of pressures yet retaining their shape, under the tension of many forces and counter-forces, and very taut much of the time.

Over and above the special significance accruing to state and local political institutions by virtue of the vital part they play on the national scene, they have drama, color, and tension that make them exciting subjects to explore in and of themselves. They are not merely marginal appendages of the over-all mechanism; they discharge important responsibilities that touch every citizen in an intimate way in the course of his daily life. For their own intrinsic fascination, then, as well as for their importance in the national political process, they warrant our attention. They are the objects of scrutiny in the chapters that follow.

A Family of Governments

The
Architecture
of State
and Local
Governments

Men build their governments as they build their houses—
in many ways, to serve many purposes. Perhaps there is in each
of these structures some basic function so vital
that the structure fails completely if that function is not adequately
performed—say shelter from the elements and from enemies
in the case of houses, maintenance of order
and protection of the group and its territory from
invasion in the case of governments. But even if these functions
are the *sine qua non* of houses and governments,

33

they by no means tell the whole story. For houses are not *merely* shelters; they are places in which to work, to breed and rear young, to play, to find peace and seclusion, to entertain and impress friends, to worship, to find release for artistic impulses, to dream, to love, and to do dozens of other things, not all of which are compatible with one another. And governments are not *simply* instruments for order and defense; they acquire symbolic significance and uses, they become means of individual and group aggrandizement, they offer services, they sometimes exploit and oppress, and they serve many other ends, both collective and individual, which frequently clash with one another. The design of houses and governments represents among other things compromises among all the competing purposes these structures might possibly fulfill. To those architects who would like to impose their own values, or their own conceptions of the best accommodation among conflicting values, on both houses and governments, the existing arrangements often seem inefficient, unlovely, and nonfunctional. To persons who prefer their own errors to the enforced wisdom of others, existing arrangements, though far from ideal, may be more attractive than someone else's utopia. So neither houses nor governments display perfect symmetry or balance; they are the products of too many adjustments and concessions for that.

In the evolution of the structure of state and local governments in the United States, there is discernible a search especially for an accommodation among three values (or objectives): representativeness; technical, nonpartisan competence; and leadership.[1] The first refers to the demand for election of public officials by some (at first) or many (later) or virtually all (a twentieth-century innovation) adult citizens over whom the officials exercise jurisdiction. The second refers to the demand for officials having training and experience qualifying them for the jobs they do, and to the insistence that their official decisions and actions be based on technical and professional considerations rather than on partisan political premises. The third refers to the demand that the actions and decisions of officials be coordinated at some central point so that government programs are reasonably consistent and efficient. These are not the only values our governmental machinery was planned to maximize, but in shaping that machinery they have been so salient that the institutions and procedures introduced into state and local governments at different stages of history, and now so familiar to us, can usefully be portrayed primarily in these terms.

At any point in history elements reflecting all three values can be discovered in our governmental system; the three are not mutually exclusive. Indeed, all have left their distinctive marks on governmental organization, with the result that governmental organization today represents a combination of devices introduced earlier and innovations constituting responses to more recent needs and desires. But at various stages of our development, one or another would receive more emphasis than the other two, partly because new conditions required new methods, partly because excessive emphasis on only one of the values tends to set in motion de-

---

[1] Herbert Kaufman, "Emerging Conflicts in the Doctrines of Public Administration," *The American Political Science Review*, Vol. L, No. 4 (December, 1956), pp. 1057–1073.

The Architecture of State and Local Governments

mands for redressing the balance. Thus without intimating that any of the values was ever completely ignored, it is possible to demonstrate that each had its heyday and left its impress on our government and politics.

State Governmental Organization and the Three Values

Nowhere is the sequence of the values more clearly illustrated than in the growth of our state governments. The early colonial period may be characterized as years of executive dominance, when governors appointed by the King of England (in the case of the crown colonies) or by the boards of directors of the companies chartered to develop and exploit the New World (in the case of the proprietary colonies), were able, with the support of the wealthier settlers, to exert considerable influence in the areas under their charge. Even in the two colonies in which the governors were elected (Connecticut and Rhode Island), the governors were almost invariably key political figures. This is not to say colonial governors were insensitive to the wishes and needs of the people under them, or indifferent to the political forces that swirled around them in their difficult assignments. But most of them were regarded as spokesmen for the mother country (in the form of the crown or the companies) and not for the people. Moreover, the colonists were not directly represented in Parliament, and parliamentary intervention in the activities of the colonists became more and more extensive as the years wore on. The situation generated resentment against both England and most of the governors, resentment that would eventually lead to revolt.

The colonies had not by any means been *without* instruments of representation. On the contrary, there were elected assemblies in all the colonies, and, although they were chosen on the basis of rather limited suffrage, they were more closely identified with the interests of the colonists than were the governors or the ruling groups in the mother country. Consequently, the assemblies in most of the colonies were widely regarded as the champions of the local populations and the foes of exploitation and arbitrary government.

Small wonder, then, that the revolution that threw off the rule of England was also directed against executive power in the colonies, while the representative branch of government—the legislature—was almost everywhere elevated to the dominant position. At the national level, antiexecutive feeling ran so high that the Articles of Confederation provided for no executive at all. (The later creation of the Presidency under the Constitution was distinctly exceptional, the defects of the Articles having induced the men at the Philadelphia convention of 1787 to go beyond their mandate and their authority, in the course of which they established a chief executive officer without parallel in any but a few of the states.) In most of the states, the governors were reduced to mere figureheads, elected by the legislatures in eleven instances,[2] chosen for one-year terms in most cases, and for the most part having negligible powers of appointment and removal, no veto, no supervisory authority, no role in the budgetary

2 Massachusetts and New York excepted.   **35**

process, no legislative function worth noting, no investigatory powers, and practically no staff aid. Virtually everything the state governments did, they did by legislative enactment. The legislatures chose the personnel of the state governments, and the administrative officials answered to the legislatures. Substantive policies of the states, state finances, and control of local governments lay in legislative hands. Even the charters of private corporations were granted by individual legislative acts. The reaction against the unrepresentativeness of pre-revolutionary government in the colonies was sweeping.

As the expanding business of the state governments in the nineteenth century compelled them to increase the size of their organizations, the pursuit of representativeness turned them in a new direction: reliance on direct election of administrative officers. This development was partly a simple extension of the logic of representativeness to its extreme; if popularly elected officials are more responsive to the electorate than are non-elected officials, then make as many of them elective as possible. Why go through the legislatures as intermediaries? Besides, the extension of the suffrage admitted to the political process a great many people who had formerly been disfranchised, and they were a little less enthusiastic than were the old dominant cliques about legislative bodies from which they had so long been excluded and which had drawn the lines of legislative constituencies to keep them that way; the newcomers had more faith in the direct election of administrative officers than in indirect election via legislatures about which they harbored some doubts. So as state governments grew, the growth included multiplication of independently elected officers, such as controllers, attorneys general, superintendents of education, other department heads, and judges. Here in fact, was the origin of the "long ballot," later to become the target of reformers; voters soon found themselves obliged to vote on scores of offices from the highest and most important down to the most trivial. (In federal elections, by contrast, voters at this time had only two choices to make: one for electors of the President and Vice President, and one for United States representative. Not until the adoption of the Seventeenth Amendment in 1913 did they get to vote for senators.) The search for representativeness may have been more ardent than wise, but the objectives were not indefensible.

At any rate, by the time of the Civil War, the triumph of this value was almost complete. Practically everywhere, state government was identified with legislative supremacy and large numbers of elective positions.

THE PURSUIT OF NONPARTISAN COMPETENCE

By the time of the Civil War, however, disillusionment had begun to set in. Legislators demonstrated they did not have a monopoly on wisdom, and some observers thought they outdid themselves in folly. In addition, partisan loyalty took precedence over fitness for position in both nominations and appointments. Whereas this situation might have been tolerable, and even laudable, in an earlier day, it created grave problems as the industrial revolution in this country transformed public servants from copyclerks into technicians and professionals. Thirdly, the knowledge that they would soon be swept out of office induced many officials to employ their period

36

of public service as an opportunity to feather their own nests; they became exceptionally susceptible to corrupting temptations in an era when slyness and amorality (if not immorality) were regarded by some business leaders as shrewdness and ingenuity, and temptations consequently abounded. Finally, citizens with political connections were able to win benefits, services, and advantages not available to their equally deserving but less favored fellows. Eventually, all these conditions exploded in a series of scandals reaching from the local level clear up to Congress, and a reaction developed. This time, however, the reaction was against the deficiencies of excessive emphasis on representativeness, just as the emphasis on representativeness had itself been a reaction against executive abuses three-quarters of a century before.

The reaction took two forms: the imposition of restrictions on the legislatures by state constitutional provisions, and a series of efforts to take entire segments of the governmental process "out of politics."

State constitutions share many attributes with the Constitution of the United States, the charters of municipal corporations, and the statutes governing unincorporated subdivisions of states. They describe the organization of the major institutions of government, basic governmental procedures, powers and limits on the powers of the occupants of the positions described, and the methods of changing the organic acts. But state constitutions occupy a unique position in theory. They do not *confer* powers on the state governments; they only *limit* the discretion of state officials. All other governments in the American system are governments of delegated powers; were it not for the authority given them by the states, they would have no legitimate authority. State governments, on the other hand, inherently have all the powers possessed by the people of the states except as they may delegate some of their powers to others or as the people of any state may choose to restrict the state government by explicit provisions written into the state constitution. Every provision of a state constitution above and beyond those provisions that deal with organizing the government tends to confine the discretion of the official positions thus established. Additions to the Constitution of the United States or to local charters or organic statutes tend frequently (but not always) to expand the powers of these governments, to broaden the delegation of power to them, to permit them to move into fields formerly barred to them, or at least to strengthen their hands in hitherto uncertain activities. Additions to the constitution of a state normally prohibit state (and sometimes local) officials from acting in ways that would lie within their discretion in the absence of such provisions. The longer a state constitution becomes, the more it circumscribes officials.

As disappointment and disillusionment with state legislatures became more intense during the nineteenth century, the constitutions therefore grew longer and longer. Some expanded to fantastic lengths; California's, for example, adopted in 1879, is more than seven times as long as the Constitution of the United States, and Louisiana's is over six times as long as the national document. Although these examples are extreme (most state constitutions are between one and a half and three times the length of the federal Constitution), they are merely exaggerations of a general tendency. State constitutions are long, and most of their content narrows the freedom of action of state officials. In particular, it restrains

The Architecture of State and Local Governments

legislatures, for it is to the legislatures that residual powers (i.e., all powers not specifically assigned to some other branch of government) fall.

So state constitutions have come to contain provisions that would astound an observer who believed they were simply small versions of the federal Constitution. In them are sections dealing in detail with public spending, taxing, and borrowing (for financial problems were among the first to beset the states after the Revolution); with local government; with the conduct of elections; with education; with corporations; with railroads; with natural resources; and with hosts of other subjects. (In one state, the flash point of diesel oil purchased by the state was specified, and the boundaries of legislative districts and of counties are often spelled out.) Admittedly, many of these details were successfully injected into the constitutions not by disinterested persons seeking to protect the general public against incompetent and untrustworthy officers, but by special interests striving for special advantages that could not be easily rescinded. Yet on balance, the trend toward greater length and specificity is clearly the result of distrust and determination to remove as much of government as possible from the hands of the very officials who had once been the great repositories of public confidence.

The other form of reaction against the consequences of unbridled pursuit of representativeness was the establishment of boards and commissions to administer new governmental functions, particularly functions of a regulatory nature. The aim of this arrangement was to reduce the influence of partisan politics, from which individual elective officials can hardly be extricated (and, it might be argued, from which they *should* not be removed). Boards and commissions were favored over single administrators because this arrangement permitted spokesmen for all the interests involved to check one another, and at the same time presumably reduced the ease with which any special interest could make bargains with administrative agencies. Indeed, to heighten the obstacles to partisan or corrupt dealing, and to assure consideration of minority points of view in policy-making, these bodies commonly were made bipartisan, with some of the seats guaranteed for the minority party. As a general rule, power of appointment was lodged in the governors, for the chief executives were the natural recipients of this responsibility as the esteem of the legislatures declined.[3] For the most part, the terms of the members were considerably longer than those of the officers who appointed them, and the expiration dates were staggered so that no one governor or legislature in a single administration could hope to replace all the members with individuals of their own choosing. Members were also protected against removal; they served not at the pleasure of the governors, but for their full terms unless they gave cause for dismissal, in which case the governors were usually required to state the cause in writing and to conduct a public hearing. Sometimes the salaries of commissioners were secured by prohibitions against reductions during their terms of office, and prospec-

[3] Other ways of constituting such boards and commissions include *ex officio* membership, by which officials appointed or elected to other offices automatically become board members; co-optation of new members by surviving members whenever vacancies occur; and restriction of the appointing officers' discretion to lists of names prepared by panels of specialists.

The Architecture of State and Local Governments

tive appointees were required to have specific technical and professional qualifications to be eligible to serve.

Having hedged the new agencies about with all these safeguards intended to assure their autonomy, the designers then felt free to endow them with considerable freedom in exercising the functions entrusted to them. Some boards and commissions were tantamount to small unifunctional legislatures, so broad was the authority delegated to them. Nearly all such bodies, even when not quite *so* generously endowed, were assigned wide discretion in discharging their responsibilities. The governmental architects of this era and their successors, their faith in the legislatures sorely shaken, turned hopefully to these new institutions to help assume the expanding burdens of an industrial society. So public-utilities commissions, banking commissions, boards of regents (for overseeing education), conservation commissions, fish and game commissions, parks councils, boards of professional licensure, tax commissions, and boards of elections all burgeoned. To be sure, the use of such bodies was by no means unknown prior to this period. Moreover, their establishment did not end with the turn of the century, for later generations employed the same device to handle labor relations, public welfare programs, and industrial planning and development, to cite the most conspicuous illustrations, when the states entered these areas. And after the Port of New York Authority was set up by agreement between New York and New Jersey in 1921, the special authority as a form appeared everywhere at the state and local levels of government. An authority is a board with power to construct and maintain facilities (bridges, tunnels, roads, etc.), to charge tolls and fees for their use and to charge rentals to businessmen who operate concessions on these properties, and to borrow against revenues to finance new facilities. They thus enjoy not only the same kinds of legal protection that other boards and commissions are afforded but also enjoy more fiscal and administrative independence from the central political organs of government. Attempts to insulate segments of government from politics, at least in part, were therefore not confined to the latter part of the nineteenth century. But in that period they certainly *began* the proliferation that was to make them a common governmental phenomenon.

The reaction against the striving for unalloyed representativeness also took what might be considered a third direction: the civil-service reform movement. The movement began prior to the Civil War, and was addressed primarily to the national government (although the spoils system it opposed was just as strongly entrenched, and had been for a longer time, within the states), perhaps because the reformers thought a national victory would usher in a wave of state and local reforms of the same character. Advocates of the merit system made some temporary gains in Washington during the Grant administration, but it was not until 1883 that they at last succeeded in procuring the enactment of the Civil Service (Pendleton) Act. From then on, personnel specialists began to displace party leaders in decisions on appointments, removals, promotions, and discipline, and another phase of governmental operations was gradually insulated from many of the political pressures to which it had originally been subject. Although the Civil Service Commission, unlike many other boards, was not especially independent in law (being under the President and serving at his pleasure until recently), it acquired considerable **39** autonomy in fact. Civil-service reform, then, may be treated as another aspect of the recoil from elections and politics.

As we have already mentioned, however, civil-service reform made comparatively limited headway at the state and local level, and much of the progress has been quite recent. Federally aided programs (certain programs of public health, welfare, vocational rehabilitation, unemployment compensation, and others) generally adopt merit systems of employment in order to qualify for federal assistance. In addition, half the states have passed laws providing general coverage, as have all large cities and most smaller ones. Outside the urban regions, formal merit system procedures are all but completely absent. Moreover, many of the statutory requirements, even where they are on the books, are not rigorously enforced and not scrupulously observed. The civil-service movement, then, is another manifestation of the anti-partisan temper of the times in which it scored its first successes, and its continued advance over the years may be interpreted as evidence of the unabated persistence of the value it reflects. But in spite of some major victories among states and localities, it has not spread nearly so widely as the other types of reaction against the aim of stressing representativeness above all else; restrictions on legislatures and establishment of relatively independent boards and commissions have been much more pervasive responses.

A new trend emerged in the twentieth century, a trend generated by dissatisfaction with the combined effects of the search for representativeness and later, reactive quest for technical competence and political neutrality. This new trend manifested itself as a hunt for ways of overcoming the fragmentation produced by the preceding governmental designers. And it settled, almost inevitably, on the governors as the solution.

Actually, the growth of gubernatorial powers began well before the turn of the century. Indeed, legislative election had given way entirely to direct election of governors soon after independence was achieved, and two-year terms rather than one-year terms became the rule, with a trend toward four-year terms soon to make an appearance. By the middle of the nineteenth century, most governors had already obtained a veto—some as strong as the President's, some more easily overridden, but a major increment to their powers in either case. The number of appointments governors could make was gradually increased. Everywhere, the governorship was rising from a purely honorific post of slight influence to a position of major importance in state government.

Still, it was not until the twentieth century that what had been a somewhat unwitting yielding to circumstances became a deliberate policy and a conscious political philosophy. By the time the first World War was upon us, state governments were thoroughly fractionized. Legislatures had proved unable to furnish leadership even when they had substantial authority; they were still less able to do so when constitutional limitations circumscribed them. Independently elected administrative officers felt no obligation to support any common program, and state policies turned into **40** a melange of unrelated and often competing or contradictory activities.

Boards and commissions conducted their own programs without reference to one another or to other governmental organs. There was little unity, little coordination, and the parties, as we saw, were in no position to supply what governmental structure did not. If the states had had no function to perform, this situation might have made little difference. But their burdens were growing, and each was organized at this stage as a group of autonomous battalions instead of as a unified army prepared to meet the challenge.

Under these conditions, both representativeness and neutral competence suffered. Most citizens who wanted to protest or overturn an action found it difficult to detect who the responsible officials were, and they were similarly frustrated when they sought to promote action. By the same token, insiders—interest groups, party personnel—could extract from individually isolated agencies practically all they wanted, because so much took place in the obscurity of the administrative jungle. Turning a party or a faction out of office seldom had profound effects on policies, partly because so much of the governmental process had already been insulated against the intervention of legislators and executives, and partly because the parties themselves were so fragmented and the lines of constituencies were so drawn that one party or faction rarely controlled the whole governmental apparatus. Anyway, most people voted blindly when confronted with the long ballots that then prevailed. All the original formulae, as they had worked out in practice, seemed to be self-defeating.[4]

Many architects of government thereupon set out in the twentieth century to make state governmental structure more orderly, rational, and visible. Their strategy was to try to reduce the autonomy of government agencies by consolidating them into great functional departments, each to be headed by an appointee of, and both legally and politically responsible to, the chief executive. The number of departments was to be held to a minimum, so that only a manageable number of subordinates would report to the governor. Constitutional and statutory sources of agency independence were to be eliminated, or at least curtailed as far as possible. The executive branch was to be turned into an administrative pyramid, with the governor at the top—and in charge.

Simultaneously, the office of governor was to be equipped for the new role it was to play. The governor was to be furnished with appropriate staff agencies that would help him plan his program and keep tabs on the way the line departments were carrying it out. Governors were also to be supplied with adequate secretarial assistance, personal aides, and advisors. Four-year terms became a target. Shorter ballots became another, so that governors would not be confronted with elected rivals whom they could not in fact control, and voters would find their electoral choices more meaningful. Executive budgets were a third target, meaning that agency requests for funds would be screened by the office of the governor and adjusted to conform with his over-all program for the state instead of going piecemeal to the legislatures where they were acted on almost haphazardly. Furthermore, the new reformers demanded the item veto for governors, so that riders (i.e., substantive legislation attached to money

4 See V. O. Key, Jr., *American State Politics: An Introduction* (New York: Knopf, 1956).

The Architecture of State and Local Governments

bills) could be returned to the legislatures without jeopardizing the entire appropriation acts to which they were appended, and so that governors could pinpoint individual "pork barrel" items in appropriations without stopping the operation of all state machinery. (The advocates of executive leadership were doubtless aware that the item veto could also be used to press individual legislators interested in particular sections of state budgets into line behind gubernatorial programs.) Gubernatorial powers of appointment and removal were to be bolstered. In short, the governorship was to be converted from an office in which an occupant might reign without ruling, in which he was neither chief nor executive, into the center of state government. He was to become an administrative and legislative leader, and therefore a political leader. This, at least, was the aim.

Progress in this direction has been uneven, as one might expect. In some states huge strides toward the reformers' ideal have been made in recent years; in most, only some of their recommendations have been followed, and rarely entirely even then. But in every state the reorganization movement has had some impact, however slight. Redesigning governmental structure and procedure is not like tinkering with the machinery of your own automobile; people develop stakes in the existing arrangements, and proposals for change have to run a long gantlet. Many proposals do not survive. Nevertheless, the reorganization movement has made its mark on American state government.[5]

While the conditions contributing to the emergence of the executive leadership value had been building up over many years, the immediate trigger seems to have been the appointment in 1910 by President Taft of a Commission on Efficiency and Economy to examine the organization and procedures of the federal government with an eye to improvement. (The report of the Commission in 1911 led to the adoption of an executive budget system by the federal government in 1921.) For the federal commission was promptly followed by governmental self-surveys in more than a dozen states. Then, in 1917, Illinois adopted a sweeping reorganization plan, and a host of states followed suit. In the next 20 years, another 25 states reorganized themselves, all but 7 comprehensively. The Illinois step is generally regarded as the breakthrough, and the starting point of the new era in the design of state governments.[6]

Another burst of state reorganizations was sparked by another federal commission, President Franklin D. Roosevelt's Committee on Administrative Management in 1937. Its report restated forcefully the premises and proposals by then associated with the reorganization movement, and over a dozen states followed this lead. In 1948 President Truman appointed a Commission on the Organization of the Executive Branch of the Government (the first "Hoover Commission," named for its chairman), and this report touched off a third wave of state reorganizations. Finally, a number of states were galvanized to action by President Eisenhower's commission on the administrative structure of the federal government (the second Hoover Commission, which reported in 1955).

As a result, the governors of all 50 states are major factors in the

[5] Cf., Jewell Cass Phillips, *State and Local Government in America* (New York: American Book Co., 1954), pp. 210–212.

[6] Cf., Leslie Lipson, *The American Governor: From Figurehead to Leader* (Chicago: University of Chicago Press, 1939).

The Architecture of State and Local Governments

politics and government of their states. None of them, it is true, is in a situation the supporters of executive leadership would consider ideal, but one has only to watch the proceedings of the national conventions to realize they are at last in a position as strong as, or perhaps even stronger than, their fellow politicians in the United States Senate. The governorship has come into its own even though there is still room for it to grow. The four-year term predominates now; 35 states have adopted it, and although many of them in some way limit their governors' eligibility to succeed themselves,[7] the chief executives have enough time to conceive and carry through at least some parts of a coherent program. Forty-one states give their governors the item veto,[8] and only one state (North Carolina) still denies its governor the legislative veto. All states authorize the governor to call special legislative sessions. Forty have adopted the executive budget. Almost everywhere, the number of departments has been reduced, while the gubernatorial power of appointment has in many cases been enlarged and even the power of removal has sometimes been augmented. Increasingly, administrative officers are expected or required to report to the governors (rather than to the legislatures). Gubernatorial staff assistance has grown considerably. The reaction to the fragmentation produced by the pursuit of different values led to a quest for administrative integration that profoundly altered the structure of state governments in a comparatively short time. It raises the question whether the next reaction will be an altogether new one or a new beginning of the same cycle.

THE RESULT: STATE GOVERNMENTAL ORGANIZATION TODAY

Evidences of the pursuit of all three values are found in the governments of the states today—even in the most recently admitted ones and those recently subjected to sweeping reorganizations. Elective state administrative offices (in addition to those of governor and lieutenant governor) have by no means disappeared entirely, nor are they likely to in the near future. Legislatures still retain substantial powers, despite the progressive curtailment of their role. On the other hand, restrictions on the frequency and duration of legislative sessions, on legislative procedure, and on the discretion of legislative bodies (in the form of mandates, prohibitions, and limitations) abound, and relatively independent boards and commissions still function almost everywhere. Yet administrative organization has been rationalized to a considerable extent, and governors are more nearly in command of their administrative machinery than ever before.

Partly because the quest for the three values was so general, and partly because the states tend to imitate one another a good deal, a person accustomed to the governmental organization of one state would not feel altogether strange if he were injected into another. The popularly elected governor and lieutenant governor, the two-house legislature (except in

[7] The most common restrictions prohibit two successive terms (but without limiting the number of separate single terms) or bar any person from holding office for more than two terms in his lifetime. Alaska bars more than two terms *in a row,* but permits ex-governors to take office again after having been out of office for at least one term.

[8] Confined almost exclusively to elimination or reduction of items from appropriations bills only.

The Architecture of State and Local Governments

Nebraska, which has adopted the unicameral form), the familiar administrative pyramid, the preservation of autonomous agencies and some elective administrative posts, the hierarchy of courts culminating in a single high judicial body with power to review legislation for consistency with the constitution, the written constitution—all these similarities would make him feel at home in any state. Yet he would be struck by differences as soon as he could probe beyond the gross outlines. He would find that all governors are not equally strong, in some instances because of differences in their constitutional authority, in others because of differences in party cohesion. (Where two parties compete on a fairly equal basis, they tend to maintain tighter discipline (thus aiding the governor) than obtains in one-party states, where the governor must bargain with recalcitrant factions that run no risk by opposing him.) He would find that 31 legislatures[9] meet only every other year, whereas 19 assemble annually; that the length of sessions is limited in 33 states to periods ranging from 36 to 150 days (with 60 days most common);[10] that a few employ a "split session," entailing an interval chiefly for introducing legislation, a recess, and a period in which legislation already introduced may be considered for passage; that special sessions are confined in most states to the subjects specified in the governor's call,[11] but not in a few states (where governors think long and hard before convening special sessions). He would find that the smallest legislative body (Nebraska, 43 members) is only a tenth the size of the largest (New Hampshire, 424), and that *area* (i.e., towns in Connecticut, New Hampshire, and Vermont) is the basis of representation in the lower house of a few legislatures whereas the *upper* house is based on population. He might find that a function assigned to a board or commission in one state is delegated to a regular department in another, and that the number of departments and agencies differs from state to state. The states are far from identical. In the light of the great variations among them in area, population, wealth, economic base, history, and other respects, it is not so remarkable that they diverge from one another to the extent they do as it is that they nevertheless retain so many similarities, one and all exhibiting structural characteristics connected with the search for representativeness, neutral competence, and executive leadership.

The Organization of Cities and the Cycle of Values

There is even less uniformity among cities than among the states, yet the effects of the three core values can also be discerned in municipal evolution and present structure. During the colonial period the governmental powers of cities were usually vested in a council, commonly elected by that

[9] The data on legislatures are drawn from The Council of State Governments, *The Book of the States, 1960–61,* Vol. XIII (Chicago: The Council of State Governments, 1960), pp. 31–58; and Legislative Drafting Fund of Columbia University, *Index Digest of State Constitutions* (New York: Oceana Press, 1959), pp. 669–671, 675, 676. See also Belle Zeller (ed.), *American State Legislatures* (New York: Crowell, 1954); and Malcolm E. Jewell, *The State Legislature: Politics and Practice* (New York: Random House, 1962).

[10] In a few states the "off-year" sessions are confined to fiscal and budgetary matters; The Council of State Governments, *The Book of the States,* Vol. XIII, p. 32.

[11] In 23 states there are limitations on the length of special sessions; *ibid.*

The Architecture of State and Local Governments

small segment of the population eligible to vote, but sometimes self-perpetuating (i.e., empowered to select the individuals to fill vacancies in their ranks). Mayors there were, to be sure, chosen by the council or by the colonial governors, and some mayors wielded considerable influence in their communities; but the position was for the most part honorific and involved little more than presiding over meetings of the council. Collectively, the council members enacted such legislation as the cities were authorized to pass. Council committees supervised the performance of administrative tasks and recommended appointments by the full council of such employees as were needed. Individually, the councilmen were often justices of the peace, and constituted a court when setting *en banc*. The structure of our early city governments was simple and clear.

The apotheosis of legislative bodies that swept through the states after the Revolution thus required no substantial changes in the cities. Modifications of form did occur; in imitation of the federal government and the states, councils were formally divided into two houses in many cities, mayors were elected directly by the voters, and the judicial function was taken away from local legislators. And the other distinguishing marks of the desire for representativeness also appeared in the first half of the nineteenth century: many municipal offices, sometimes down to dog-catcher, were filled by election; all terms were made short, to encourage rotation in office; the franchise was gradually extended, and organized political parties appeared on the scene. Nevertheless, the dominance of the councils in the formal organization of city governments was not disturbed. If anything, the councils gained strength as new responsibilities were thrust on cities by growing populations and accelerating industrialization.

At the city level as at the state level, and for the same reasons, there was a post-Civil-War recoil from the emphasis on representativeness. It is doubtful that there was ever a time when the Jacksonian belief that any citizen could be relied on to perform the duties of public service (in the same way that amateurs are called on to serve as jurors) was completely valid. At any rate, this notion was certainly out of place as governments were compelled to engage in highly technical operations on a large scale in the latter part of the nineteenth century, and as businessmen amassed vast aggregations of capital, parts of which they were not averse to use for influencing parties and public officials. City governments were not always up to these new demands. There were, as in the state governments, wholesale surrenders to the blandishments of traction companies, public utilities, and other special interests. "Rings" of politicians used their intervals in office to enrich themselves and their friends. Reform groups therefore sought to curtail the role of the parties in municipal government, to isolate as much of the political process as they could from partisan politicians, to put government in the hands of officials and employees who would be neutral with respect to the parties and experts in their work. The search for representativeness gave way to the quest for nonpartisan competence.

The methods of achieving this objective were the same in the cities as in the states. Reformers demanded and obtained new state statutory restrictions on the discretion of municipal legislative bodies (although it was not long before they were to pick up the banners of "home rule"). In some of the larger cities, merit systems were introduced. Almost everywhere, new functions were entrusted to agencies headed by boards or

The Architecture of State and Local Governments

commissions whose members had long, overlapping terms, sometimes were appointed by governors, occasionally were self-perpetuating, but in every case had broad and almost autonomous powers over the activity within their purview. Governmental machinery, already sundered by the advocates of unrestrained representativeness, was further splintered.

Toward the end of the nineteenth century, the supporters of executive leadership were urging their doctrines at the city level. Fragmentation of government, they argued, did not weaken party influence; on the contrary, it intensified the power of party officers because it made dealing with the government too complicated and uncertain, whereas one could reach agreements with party bosses who would then handle the arrangements with all the separate institutions of a municipality. Moreover, it strengthened special interest groups, which reached agreements with the agencies that concerned them without having to defend their particularistic claims in the broader arena of public policy formation. What is more, fractionizing government led to conflicts, contradictions, and confusion among officials, so that regulations and services duplicated one another, or clashed, or were neglected by officials unable to agree on whose responsibilities they were. In the cities as at the higher levels of government, integration, coordination, and unity under the leadership of the chief executive became battle cries, and reforms intended to build up the position of the mayor gained momentum.

The strategies for accomplishing these ends, as we have already mentioned, were the same in the cities as at the higher governmental levels. Mayors' terms were lengthened. Their powers of appointment and removal were broadened. Many obtained the veto. In larger cities mayors were charged with formulating and executing the municipal budgets. Their staffs were increased. During the present century, as the federal government and the states modified their structure in order to strengthen the leadership of their chief executives, many cities have followed suit. The movement went on at all governmental echelons simultaneously.

Advances in this direction have by no means been universal among municipalities, however. In all cities with mayors and councils, traces of the earlier values persist; indeed, not many mayoralties have kept pace with the growth of the governorships and the Presidency. Independently elected officers and comparatively autonomous boards and commissions still abound. Two-year terms are still very common. Mayoral financial authority is often hedged with crippling limitations. As a matter of fact, the nineteenth-century pattern is still so widespread that many writers of political science textbooks refer to it as the "weak-mayor and council" form of city government in contrast with the more modern "strong-mayor" form. These forms are better regarded as positions on a continuum, though, than as mutually exclusive classes, for it is quite obvious that cities range in fact from one extreme to the other; indeed, there is no specific ideal type of either form. What is more, many a city with a "weak" mayor in terms of formal powers has elected a man who in practice dominates the government and politics of the town, whereas many an occupant of a "strong" mayoralty turns out to be hemmed in and immobilized by the political forces around him. So the ordinary terminology of municipal government should be used and interpreted with caution. What

The Architecture of State and Local Governments

the distinction points up is that the fragmentation of city governments during the ascendancy of representativeness and then of nonpartisan competence has by no means disappeared in the present day. Progress toward executive leadership has been spotty and erratic. But the evidence of such progress is undeniable. Changes in cities have been less dramatic than changes in the states, but the changes have been the same in kind even if smaller in magnitude.

The quest for integration of municipal governments took an unusual turn during the early part of the twentieth century. While most cities, the states, and the federal government selected the chief executive as the means to this end, a number of cities completely abandoned the separation of powers. In a few decades their example was followed by hundreds of cities throughout the country.

The initial reorganization of this kind took place in Galveston, when a tidal wave and flood devastated that city. The government in power, which had been under criticism for its weaknesses even before the disaster, was utterly unable to cope with the emergency. A group of businessmen thereupon recommended drastic modifications, and the state legislature granted a charter embodying their proposals. In 1901 the new plan took effect, and the government of Galveston passed into the hands of a body of five officials, three appointed by the governor and two elected by the voters. Four of the five were in charge of individual city departments; one served as mayor, but, under the circumstances, he was primarily a presiding and a ceremonial officer. Collectively, the commission exercised the legislative powers of the city and jointly made all major appointments and other decisions. Such was the revulsion against the consequences of earlier values that almost every trace of them was eliminated. Representativeness was almost totally suppressed, and the separate boards and commissions were abolished. This was executive government at its peak, and the "commission plan" (as it came to be known) came closer to the colonial pattern than any other modern form.

It was not long before the older values reasserted themselves within the new framework. Within a couple of years, in Galveston itself, all the commissioners were made elective. A few years later Des Moines added nonpartisan nominations and elections (i.e., primary elections followed by general run-off elections for the front-runners in the primaries without party designations appearing anywhere on either primary or general election ballots); the initiative (allowing introduction of legislation by circulation of petitions among voters); the referendum (requiring approval of proposed legislation by the voters in an election); the recall (permitting a substantial minority of voters by petition to compel a new election for an office occupied by an incumbent with whom they are dissatisfied); and the merit system for most city employees. All these innovations were designed to weaken the position of party organizations in municipal affairs. So past values would not be wholly denied. Nevertheless, the radical departure from traditional forms represented a triumph of executive institutions that supporters of traditional chief executives probably never visualized and certainly did not advocate.

The commission form of government spread rapidly up to the years preceding World War I; since the war, although adopted in a few cities

The Architecture of State and Local Governments

in the course of each decade, the movement has been losing ground both relatively and absolutely as cities go over to other governmental forms. There have been many variations on the commission form, permitting adaptation to local tastes. In some cities, for example, the mayor is the commissioner with the highest number of votes; in others, he is chosen by his colleagues; in still others, the candidates for mayor run for the designated office only. In general, each commissioner designates the department for which he runs, but sometimes the departments are allocated among the commissioners at their first meeting after election. Commissions range in size from 3 to 9 members. The flexibility of the plan, though, has not been sufficient to sustain it. The frequent deadlocks among the commissioners, with no easy way of breaking such paralysis; the neglect of minority interests of all kinds in a system without the protections afforded by checks and balances; the underemphasis on values which still had great appeal to many segments of the population; and the competition from other forms of municipal government not afflicted with such defects, all combined to diminish the attractiveness of the commission plan. It has passed its zenith, and will doubtless one day be widely regarded as what it is already considered by some to be: an aberrational form engendered by the reactions to earlier stress on representativeness and nonpartisan competence, brought into being by a strange series of interconnected events, and adopted because of a blind tendency to imitate that has so often been displayed in American state and local politics.

Perhaps the chief significance of the commission plan may turn out to be its part in developing another municipal form of government that lacks separate legislative and executive branches—the "council-manager" form. The commission form was winning converts in city after city when the National Short Ballot Association was formed in 1908 to press for a reduction of the number of elective offices in American government. In the same year Staunton, Virginia, which was prevented by provisions of the state constitution and laws from adopting the commission plan and instead had appointed a general manager under its mayor-council form, reported great improvements in municipal administration as a result of concentrating extensive administrative authority (including budgetary powers) in this official. Richard S. Childs, a leader of the short ballot movement, saw in the two institutions—i.e., the small commission and the general manager—a chance to achieve both a short ballot and executive leadership by an expert, professionally trained manager. He persuaded the Board of Trade of Lockport, New York, to sponsor a charter combining the two institutions in 1911, providing for a small elected council with authority to hire and fire a powerful manager at will. Although the charter was disapproved by the state legislature, the publicity focused attention on the new proposal. A few cities in other states adopted it soon afterwards, and then Dayton, Ohio, instituted it in 1914, in the wake of a disastrous flood. From then on, it gained adherents in droves until today more cities between 10,000 and 500,000 population employ the council-manager form than the mayor-council form, with additional cities joining the ranks every year. An International City Managers Association was formed as early as 1914, adopted a code of ethics for managers by 1924, and now has a membership exceeding 2,800, of whom more than 1,400 are active managers. There is a National Municipal League that pushes the manager plan, and a number of universities now offer graduate training specifically for persons who select city management as careers.[12]

Thus, in just a few decades, a new form of city government was designed and introduced, and bids fair in the years ahead to become the principal type of urban government in America. Comparisons are frequently drawn between city managers and the general managers of corporations, who serve at the pleasure of their boards of directors. But it would not be amiss to suggest a very rough parallel with the prime minister of a parliamentary government, who serves until he can no longer command a legislative majority. To be sure, a prime minister is ordinarily the leader of the majority party, whereas a city manager is supposed to be a nonpolitical figure who accepts policy instructions from his council. In theory, he is the embodiment of political neutrality and professional competence. In fact, the very nature of their positions obliges city managers to formulate policy proposals for council consideration and to guide them through the legislative process the way other public executives do. Moreover, the managers' broad powers of appointment and removal, of supervision of administrative agencies, of budget preparation and execution, as well as their visibility in the community and their opportunities to establish key contacts and mobilize community opinion often make them forces to be reckoned with. Whatever the mythology of the designers of this plan, managers are not simple tools of the councilmen. (A mayor in a council-manager city is essentially a presiding officer and ceremonial chief who is elected by the other councilmen or is the councilman who receives the highest number of popular votes). Representativeness (through the council), nonpartisan competence, and executive leadership (the last two through the manager) have left their marks on the council-manager form as well as on the more traditional forms, although the emphasis on the last two is far greater than on the first.

The council-manager plan has made little headway in the nation's largest cities. Of 17 cities over 500,000 in population, only one (Cincinnati) has adopted and retained it, while another (Cleveland) tried it and rejected it. In America's great metropolises, the mayor-council form holds undisrupted sway.[13] Yet the advantages of professionally qualified managerial assistance have not been lost on them. Unwilling to relinquish the great opportunities for needed political leadership that an independently elected chief executive alone can provide, and at the same time eager to avail themselves of the benefits of technical administrative skills, several cities since the 1930's have adopted an arrangement intended to capitalize on both the mayoralty and the managership plans. Variously referred to as the mayor-manager form, the mayor-administrator form, and the mayor-

[12] A very brief history of the manager plan is contained in National Municipal League, *The Story of the Council Manager Plan* (New York: National Municipal League, 1940). See also Jewell Cass Phillips, *Municipal Government and Administration* (New York: Macmillan, 1960), pp. 307–316, and the references cited on p. 230. The other data presented in the discussion above are drawn from International City Managers' Association, *The Municipal Year Book* (Chicago, 1961), pp. 76, 493.

[13] Bicameral councils, however, have almost everywhere given way to unicameral bodies in the course of the twentieth century, and the size of even the unicameral bodies has tended to decrease. Charles M. Kneier, *City Government in the United States*, 3rd ed. (New York: Harper, 1957), pp. 220–222.

The Architecture of State and Local Governments

chief administrative officer (CAO) form, the arrangements are by no means uniform.[14] They do, however, share one major characteristic: the mayor is always retained as chief executive and is furnished with an administrative officer responsible to him and invested with extensive authority over the managerial aspects of governmental operations. In San Francisco, one of the first cities to install this machinery, the mayor appoints the chief administrative officer, but may not remove him; only two-thirds of the board of supervisors (i.e., the council), or the voters by means of a popular recall, can do so. On the other hand, although the CAO's authority over administration is considerable, and includes power to appoint and remove the heads of agencies under his jurisdiction, a number of major departments, including police, fire, welfare, personnel, and law, are not under his supervision. In Philadelphia the managing director's tenure is not so secure, for he is appointed for a four-year term coinciding with the mayor's, may be removed by the mayor at any time, and may appeal to the civil-service commission for the balance of his salary but not for reinstatement if he believes the removal was without good cause. He is clearly the "mayor's man." At the same time, virtually all the departments serving the people directly are under his supervision and subject to his control. The governmental architects in Philadelphia thus hoped to take full advantage of the skills of the managing director without making him a rival of the mayor. New Orleans comes close to the Philadelphia pattern, but New York rejected similar recommendations by a state committee studying its organization and instead created a city administrator without powers of appointment, removal, and close supervision. Other large cities make still other provisions. Thus this "plan" of city government is far from standardized and its future is not easily assessed. But it is an interesting manifestation of the twentieth-century trend toward strengthened executive leadership, and of the desire to preserve the institutions making for representativeness and political direction while also maximizing the values of neutral competence. Ideally, this form would assure professional expertise in the conduct of administrative detail and free the mayor to concentrate on the burning problems of policy and politics that are his prime obligations and the real determinants of his own and his city's future.

In general terms, then, our cities in much the same fashion as our states have been organized around three core values, and the sequence of emphasis on each of the values has been roughly parallel in both levels of government. In the cities, however, the most recent quest for executive leadership has taken several directions rather than just one. Along with the efforts to build up mayors for this task have come the commission form and the city manager. The latter in particular is certain to challenge the mayor as the instrument of leadership in all but the largest urban areas. Whether the growth of executive power will again occasion alarm,

[14] Cf., Jewell Cass Phillips, *Municipal Government and Administration* (New York: Macmillan, 1960), pp. 323–330; Charles K. Adrian, *Governing Urban America*, 2nd ed. (New York: McGraw-Hill, 1961), pp. 210–214; Temporary [New York] State Commission to Study the Organizational Structure of the Government of the City of New York, *Four Steps to Better Government of New York City* (1953), Part 1, pp. 14–17, 31–51; Part 2, pp. 12–17; Wallace S. Sayre, "The General Manager Idea for Large Cities," *Public Administration Review*, Vol XIV (Autumn, 1954), pp. 253 ff.

The Architecture of State and Local Governments

Population	Total Number of U.S. Cities	Total Number of Cities in Table	Mayor-Council		Commission		Council-Manager	
			No.	%[a]	No.	%[a]	No.	%[a]
Over 500,000	20	20	16	80.0	0	0	4	20.0
250,000–500,000	30	30	13	43.3	5	16.7	12	40.0
100,000–250,000	80	80	30	37.5	11	13.8	39	48.8
50,000–100,000	192	190	67	35.3	27	14.2	96	50.5
25,000–50,000	405	388	132	34.0	51	13.1	205	52.8
10,000–25,000	1,030	1,005	499	49.7	101	10.0	405	40.3
5,000–10,000	1,290	1,257	838	66.7	66	5.2	353	28.1
All cities over 5,000	3,047	2,970[b]	1,595	53.7	261	8.8	1,114	37.5

[a] Percentage of total number of cities in this table in each population class.
[b] Does not include Washington, D.C., 15 cities with town meeting government, 19 cities with representative town meeting government, and 43 cities for which no information was obtained.
Source: International City Managers' Association, *The Municipal Year Book, 1961* (Chicago, 1961), p. 76.

whether new forms will emerge, whether new values will be added, remain to be seen. The drama of governmental evolution is not likely to end with any given type of organization.

Non-urban Governments Contrasted with Chartered, Incorporated Forms

The process of governmental evolution has been much slower in non-urban areas than in cities. Neither technical competence nor strong leadership were essential to communities in which governments were confined to few functions and services; the old Jacksonian ideal of rotation of the general public in office could be more or less honored. Where no urban explosion occurred, traditional patterns of governmental organization continued to serve adequately, and stability rather than change prevailed. Such communities felt no call to experiment in the fashion of cities.

A city is a municipal corporation. That is to say, it is a group of people who collectively have certain powers, rights, privileges, and obligations defined in a charter granted by the sovereign (the state, in this case). This definition of a corporation is not complete, but it will suffice for our purposes here. In some states, some municipal corporations are legally called boroughs, and smaller communities may sometimes be organized as incorporated villages having fewer powers and obligations than cities. "City," though, is the most widespread term for municipal corporations of general governmental authority. And the reasons for incorporation are to obtain the powers that go with it, powers enabling a populace to adapt its government and its public policies to its own needs and preferences.

Not all the powers and obligations of a municipal corporation are ordinarily to be found in the document formally labeled as its charter. For local governments are creations of the states and are always subject to state control (in spite of state constitutional provisions to the contrary, as we saw earlier). Consequently, a person who wants to know all the things the officers of his city may do, must do, and must not do, will have to consult a wide array of state laws in addition to the charter (which has the same general status as a state statute). For example, city officials will

The Architecture of State and Local Governments

be governed by the state education law, public health law, public works law, civil service law, and many others. But it is the charter, explicit or tacit, that almost always is the symbol and the basis of the corporation.

Originally, each municipal charter was an individual, special act of the state legislature. Later, when city rebellion against legislative intervention in urban affairs produced prohibitions against legislation addressed to specific cities (except when requested by the cities), charters were given more general form, and a community, by going through the prescribed procedures, would adopt the general charter for cities of its size, or might choose among different optional charters provided for cities of its size. Still later, under home-rule laws, a community might frame and adopt its own charter under procedures set out in constitution or statutes. City charters therefore are rarely identical; in greater or lesser degree, they are tailored to the needs of the populace to which they apply.

Municipal corporations consequently function in a dual capacity. Created by the state for the convenience of the state, they are instruments for accomplishing state purposes. Requested by the people they govern, they are also instruments for local service. In their former capacity they share some of the state's powers and immunities (e.g., immunity from suit); in the latter capacity, they are in much the same position as private corporations. In practice, however, this distinction is not sharp and may even be disappearing as new statutes and judicial interpretations modify traditional doctrines. What the states say, more than custom or common law or inherent rights, determines the status of municipal corporations. By the terms and conditions in the charters and in laws that apply to all municipal corporations, the states have granted them authority and also

Table 12   URBAN POPULATION IN THE UNITED STATES (in thousands) In Selected Years

Year	Total United States Population	Urban Population	
		No.	% of Total
1800	5,308	322	6.1
1840	17,069	1,845	10.8
1860	31,443	6,217	19.8
1900	75,995	30,160	39.7
1920	105,711	54,158	51.2
1960	179,323	125,269	69.8

Source: Statistical Abstract of the United States, 1961 (82nd ed., Washington, 1961), pp. 5, 22, 26.

imposed requirements; it is necessary in each case to examine these terms and conditions, for the general rule of "dual capacity" is at best a very rough and sometimes misleading guide.

About two-thirds of the population of the United States live in incorporated municipalities. Many of these municipalities, to be sure, are very small—indeed, have fewer than a thousand residents—and some were organized in order to forestall annexation by larger and rapidly expanding cities nearby. Yet even if we give them the benefit of any ambiguities of definition and call them municipalities, that still leaves one-

The Architecture of State and Local Governments

third of the population dependent on other forms of local government for their local services and regulation. By the most conservative estimate, a very substantial proportion of the American people live entirely under unincorporated general governments, mostly in rural sections.[15]

Where there is no incorporated government (and, in the case of the very small municipalities, even where there is one), the people are served mainly by counties (found virtually everywhere in the country), or by towns or townships (common in 22 states), or by combinations of the two.[16] These divisions are usually supplemented by special districts of various kinds, discussed below.

The theoretical distinction between the unincorporated governments and the municipal corporations is that the former are supposed to be roughly equivalent to administrative districts of the states rather than to independent units of self-government. They do not have charters (except in a few very rare instances, and then they are indistinguishable from cities), they are organized under general laws and statutes originally drafted by the states rather than by local interests, their powers and privileges are normally narrower than those of corporations, and their immunities are usually broader because they are primarily state agents. Actually, however, when we examine closely those counties (almost 80 of them) with more than 250,000 people, the line between the categories blurs, and the discrimination of incorporated from unincorporated governments reduces itself to fine points of law.

It is not easy to describe the structure of unincorporated units, either, for the patterns are so diverse. In New England, for example, although counties exist formally in four states, they perform so few functions as to

[15] U.S. Bureau of the Census, *1957 Census of Governments*, Vol. I, No. 1, "Governments in the United States" (1957), pp. 1–2.

[16] "*Municipalities:* A municipality, for purposes of census statistics, is a political subdivision of a state within which a municipal corporation has been established to provide general local government for a specific population in a defined area. A municipality may be designated as a city, borough, village, or town except in the New England states, New York, and Wisconsin. There, the term 'town' relates to an area subdivision of the county or state which, although it usually has a corresponding governmental organization and may be legally termed a municipal corporation, only incidentally relates to a population concentration. In addition to towns of the New England type, 'charter' counties also are excluded from the census classification of municipalities, as are incorporated townships of the New Jersey and Pennsylvania types. Many townships and New England towns serve population concentrations, but these are individual members of a class which, if included in the classification of municipalities, would embrace the entire area, rural and urban, of the states concerned.

"*Townships:* Under this general heading are included 'towns' in the six New England states and in New York and Wisconsin, 'plantations' and 'locations' in Maine and New Hampshire, and governments called 'townships' in other states. The vast majority of townships are rural local governments serving area subdivisions of the counties. Townships are distinguished from municipalities in that they exist to serve inhabitants of a defined area without regard to population concentrations. Most townships perform a limited range of governmental functions. However, in the New England states, New Jersey, and Pennsylvania, to a lesser extent in New York and Wisconsin, and for urban areas in some other states, towns and townships are permitted to provide a range of services which may approach that of municipalities." U.S. Bureau of the Census, *Local Government Structures in the United States* (State and Local Government Special Studies, No. 34, 1954), p. 6. Cf., also, the reference cited in Note 15.

The Architecture of State and Local Governments

be negligible; and in the other two (Connecticut and Rhode Island), they are nonexistent as units of government. In a number of middle Atlantic states and some north central states, the counties are quite vigorous, but they share their responsibilities with townships within their borders, and their governing bodies are made up of representatives from each of the townships. In several southern and border states, judges preside over county boards consisting of elected justices of the peace. In the West small boards of commissioners, elected at large or from districts or from combinations of these, are the key officials. The largest county boards consist of as many as 150 members; most, however, have from 3 to 5 members. In general, the county boards not only make policy decisions of a legislative nature (including the raising and expenditure of funds) but jointly appoint and supervise the county personnel who administer these decisions, although they commonly are confronted with independently elected officials (county clerks, registrars, auditors, treasurers, for instance) with whom the powers of the county are divided. In those counties with rapidly increasing populations and expanding lists of activities, it is now common to strengthen the presiding officer of the board, or even to appoint a county manager or executive, responding to the same problems with the same solutions as the cities and states. As a general rule, though, counties are governed without any real chief executives, with power split up among several elected administrators. In this respect they reflect the dominant value of the first half of the nineteenth century.

So, too, do the towns and townships. Indeed, the New England town meeting, comprising every eligible voter in the town, and often described as the cradle of democracy, still persists in many towns, and the only concession many other towns in this region have made to growing populations and waning attendance is to adopt representative town-meeting systems (consisting of elected delegates instead of the voters themselves). Between meetings, boards of selectmen, boards of finance, and other officials, appointive and elective, handle the business of the towns. Only in a few places have towns yielded to the trends of recent times and appointed professionally qualified managers to serve under the boards. Otherwise, where the towns have not incorporated, the institutions remain today essentially as they were a century ago.[17]

In other states where townships function as local units of government, some provide for township meetings on the New England model while others now vest responsibility for government directly in township boards. About half have strengthened the chief officer (variously called supervisor, trustee, or chairman), but all retain a relatively long list of independently elected administrative officers as well. Instead of attempting to modernize these units of government to meet the demands of the modern day, some states have begun to transfer their functions to the counties in which they are located. Township government is clearly declining. Time, and the changing values of new generations, have passed it by.

Many counties, towns, and townships in non-urban areas have been able to survive with little change, because these areas have somehow escaped, ignored, or resisted the pressures to which the federal government,

[17] Cf., Clyde F. Snider, *Local Government in Rural America* (New York: Appleton-Century-Crofts, 1957), Chapters 8, 9.

The Architecture of State and Local Governments

the states, and the cities (as well as urbanized counties) have been forced to respond with reorganization and structural experimentation. Non-urban governments were by and large content to perform only those functions they originally assumed when America was an agricultural country subscribing to the slogan that that government is best which governs least. Building and maintaining roads (so farmers could take their produce to market), providing rudimentary kinds of law enforcement and judicial administration, furnishing simple kinds of relief (going back to the days of Elizabeth I in England), and raising just enough money to pay for these activities were the extent of their responsibilities, and so remain up to the present day. Public health, modern welfare programs, public hospitals, land-use regulation, control and encouragement of housing, public sanitation, professional fire protection, construction and administration of parks and other recreational facilities, public libraries, and all the other functions necessitated by heavy concentrations of population and industry, these units of governments did not have to assume. So they made no effort to find technical, nonpartisan competence in officials and felt no urgent deficiencies in the lack of forceful executive leadership. The values of an earlier era remained valid for them, and so did the political machinery that reflected those values and no others.

Already, suburban areas have had to make adjustments; the old machinery could not withstand the strains generated by the metropolitan explosions following World War II, and drastic revisions are becoming the order of the day. Eventually, the new problems and the new values will probably reach even into those sections now almost wholly rural in character. Perhaps they will then run the same cycle as those other governments that have already been challenged by twentieth-century demands. On the other hand, perhaps they will give way entirely to newer forms. At any rate, in the next generation, if not in this one, the non-urban governments of America are sure to undergo sweeping changes, and the repercussions will ultimately be felt both in state and national politics.

Special Districts and Authorities and the Core Values

Our non-urban forms of government were shaped largely by only one of the three values discernible in the development of our city, state, and federal governments. The abundance of special districts and authorities stems partly from a search for two of these values: representativeness and nonpartisan technical competence. For in the creation of these agencies, there are few evidences of concern for enhancing the authority of elected chief executives. If anything, there are signs of downright hostility toward all branches of general governments.[18]

School districts are the most striking examples. Over four-fifths of all the public schools in the country are operated by independent school districts, which is to say by independently elected school boards with authority to levy taxes and float bonds to pay for their school systems, to

[18] General governments is the generic term for those units of government not restricted to one or a few functions. It refers chiefly to towns, counties, cities, states, and the federal government, in contrast to special units of government, such as school districts, sanitary districts, highway "authorities," and so on, which are limited to the specific duties described by their titles.

The Architecture of State and Local Governments

construct and staff the schools, to decide how far above state-prescribed minimum standards they want to go, and to set other educational policies within the limits established by state education law. State educational laws, it is true, are everywhere quite detailed, and state educational authorities normally do not hesitate to intervene in districts in which they believe state statutes and administrative regulations are not being properly executed. Nevertheless, school boards enjoy broad areas of discretion over the direction, emphasis, and quality of public education, and over the financing of school systems; and they are empowered in most cases to make their decisions without obligatory reference to local units of general government operating in much the same territory and serving some or all of the same people. In other words, they are local units of government confined to only one function, education. In 29 states, this is to all intents and purposes the only way schools up to the twelfth grade are administered, and in 15 additional states this method is extensively but not exclusively employed. In only 4 states is the management of the schools entirely in the hands of general local governments (i.e., cities, counties, towns) whose officials finance and supervise public education as they do police, fire, sanitation, and other governmental functions. All in all, there are over 50,000 independent school districts in the United States, but if they seem extraordinarily numerous now, the trends of the times are indicated by the fact that there were twice as many only 20 years ago.[19] They are rapidly being consolidated in all states in which they exist. This changes their size, however, not their form; there are fewer of them today but they are no less independent.

School districts were instituted early in the nineteenth century as a way of assuring local control and of facilitating the construction in every community of schools children could walk to in all sorts of weather. Later, as population density increased and general governments took on more and more functions, suggestions that education might be transferred to the general governments met with resistance. School districts would, it was alleged, become "involved in politics" if education officers had to compete with administrators from other departments and agencies for attention and support. Educational administrators, teachers, and schools of education developed the attributes, ethos, aspirations, and demands common to other professional groups and opposed the intrusion of laymen into a field in which they were presumably experts. The elected school boards tended to become their instruments rather than their masters, so the professionals effectively gained control of their function. Moreover, they were not anxious to risk interference by party leaders and other outsiders so conspicuously active in the management of general governments. "Keep education out of politics" became the battle cry; by inference, one may detect an unspoken corollary in the argument: "leave it to the experts." In most places this plea for autonomy by the specialists was successful. Neutral competence was to be preserved by separation and insulation from the rest of government, just as representativeness was protected by electing the boards. Leadership by the chief executives of general governments, however, was ignored and even deliberately avoided.

[19] The statistics are from U.S. Bureau of the Census, *1957 Census of Governments*, Vol. I, No. 1, "Governments in the United States" (1957), pp. 3–6. See Table 1 for additional data and sources.

The Architecture of State and Local Governments

Although school districts are declining in number, other types of special districts have been increasing rapidly.[20] There are about 14,000 of them today, most of them, like school districts, administering a single function (e.g., fire protection, soil conservation, drainage, or housing), a few performing several related functions (such as water supply, sanitation, irrigation, and flood control). For the most part they are creations of convenience, designed to facilitate service across existing political boundary lines, to evade tax and debt limitations that apply to general governments, or to operate with more flexibility than can an ordinary department of a general government. The boards of many of these special districts are elected, but many others are appointed by county judges or other officials and some consist of members *ex officio* (i.e., members who are on the boards by virtue of holding some other office). Representativeness here does not receive the same stress we have seen elsewhere, but response to the clamor for "nonpolitical" administration and insulation of a function from the normal play of political forces is even more in evidence here than in other instruments of local government.

This is especially true of those special districts managed by boards officially designated "authorities," of which the Port of New York Authority, established in 1921, is the prototype. No authorities have elective boards; appointment by the governor is probably the most common pattern, although some mayors also possess this power with respect to some authorities. This reliance on appointment rather than election may be regarded as yet another symptom of the disillusionment with the electoral process and with the politics it entails.

As a rule authorities are established for the same reasons as other special districts—convenience and flexibility. But they normally have no taxing power. For income they depend entirely on revenues from the facilities they operate, such as toll bridges, toll roads, airports, and the like, and on the money they are able to borrow against future earnings. In addition to their fiscal freedom, they also enjoy a greater measure of administrative autonomy than ordinary agencies of general governments. Many have followed the lead of the Port of New York Authority and established salary scales that enable them to compete with private industry for managerial talent, with the result that, like the Port Authority, they have established outstanding records of efficiency, integrity, and accomplishment. Let anyone suggest, however, that perhaps the functions they perform should be brought under the control of general governments so that the total pattern of governmental investment and expenditure could be shaped on an integrated basis rather than by a series of *ad hoc* decisions and they protest, not without justification, that they will soon fall prey to partisan politics. Like the professional educators, they contend they want to keep their activities out of politics, which means they want to maintain their specialists in control of the policies within their jurisdiction. They prefer the politics of experts to the politics of parties. In this sense the specialized authorities represent the fullest development in the American polity of machinery for maximizing nonpartisan competence.

Thus, the values pursued by the architects of governments in the nineteenth century have by no means been abandoned today; they are

[20] *Ibid.,* pp. 6–7.

The Architecture of State and Local Governments

mirrored in recently invented institutions as well as in older ones. Nor are they likely to disappear. Yet just as their values fragmented general governments at the state and local level and thereby touched off a movement to strengthen the powers of chief executives, so they are now generating questions about the fractionization caused by the proliferation of special districts. Whether this reaction will give added impetus to the search for general executive leadership or will take some other direction remains to be seen. What can be perceived now, albeit in rather dim outline, is the gathering of opposing forces.

Courts and the Core Values

The organization of our state judicial systems, no less than the structure of the other branches of government, has been molded by the quest for the core values. And our judicial systems, like our special districts, have been built around the first two values rather than around all three. It seems strange to persons reared in Anglo-Saxon juridical traditions even to intimate that control of the judiciary should be vested in our chief executives. Yet in most European countries, the judiciary is located in an executive department, the Ministry of Justice, and judges are appointed civil servants. If America and England resort to different practices, it is not because any alternative is inconceivable or necessarily inconsistent with democracy; rather, it is because these two nations sought some different values.

In the colonial period English judges at all levels were appointed by the crown, and this system was introduced into the New World (albeit with the colonial governors acting as the actual appointing officers). After the Revolution old hostilities toward the executive branch manifested themselves in provisions for legislative appointment of judges in many states. Then, in the first half of the nineteenth century, came the spread of the Jacksonian faith in the electoral process (a faith amplified by the conviction on the part of the poorer people that the judiciary of the era was consistently unsympathetic to them), and there was a pronounced swing toward making judgeships elective. Today, all judges in 21 states, and all but the judges of inferior courts in 14 more, are popularly elected. Four states still cling to legislative election in picking judges. Gubernatorial or local executive appointment prevails in the remaining states, but almost always with some form of confirmation by one or both houses of the legislature, by a panel of experts, or by some other body. Three states require the governors' appointees to face election on their records after having served for a certain period. Representativeness in our judiciary thus remains one of our prominent goals.[21]

Inevitably, election of judges led to the development of strong links between the parties and the judiciary,[22] just as it led to close ties between the parties and the other branches of government. Courts, in fact, became especially important to the party organizations. Because judgeships carry

[21] Cf., Jewell Cass Phillips, *State and Local Government in America* (New York: American Book Co., 1954), p. 238; William Anderson, Clara Penniman, and Edward W. Weidner, *Government in the 50 States* (New York: Holt, Rinehart and Winston, 1960), p. 290.

[22] See Wallace S. Sayre and Herbert Kaufman, *Governing New York City* (New York: Russell Sage Foundation, 1959), Chapter XIV.

The Architecture of State and Local Governments

prestige, substantial salaries, good working conditions, long tenure, attractive opportunities for advancement up the judicial ladder, and influence in political and professional circles, they are eagerly sought by members of the bar. Consequently, the parties are reasonably sure of a supply of precinct workers and of legal talent. Also, judges grateful for past favors or hopeful of future ones are frequently substantial contributors to party fund-raising affairs, and so are many others who would like to become judges. Moreover, judges are themselves appointing officers, what with their official staffs and court aides to name, and rarely are there any merit system procedures to hamper their exercise of discretion. To the parties the judicial system means non-judicial as well as judicial jobs to dispense. In addition, judges of some courts select referees, guardians, executors of estates, and the like, and these positions can be highly remunerative for those who win them. In short, the judicial system is a source of many of the rewards and incentives that hold the parties together.

At the same time, the parties are important to judges and would-be judges. Although party leaders must take into account the demands and requests of all kinds of influential groups in their communities (since to alienate too many of these interests can cost the party votes and donations and volunteer workers), they play the key role in selecting candidates for elective positions. Even the introduction of the direct primary has not dislodged them from their principal role in this process. Ordinarily, party members loyal to party leaders (or to leaders of factions) rather than "independents" in the party ranks determine the results of primaries. Furthermore, executives empowered to appoint judges customarily use their authority to build party following and unity, and to assemble legislative support for their programs, so they will not casually disregard the advice and recommendations of party leaders. Consequently, judges anxious to hold their places when their terms are up, or to advance to higher courts, as well as aspirants who hope for nomination or appointment to the bench, cultivate the favor of the party organizations.

The parties also conduct campaigns for their judicial candidates, and this has particular significance because vigorous campaigning of the sort we take for granted on the part of nominees for the legislature and executive posts is somehow considered inconsistent with the nature of judicial office. Even more than their running mates, therefore, nominees for court positions are dependent on party organizations to obtain votes for them; they urgently need the party label and party publicity efforts.

Finally, party leaders rather than judges spearhead the drive for pay increases for the judiciary and for increases in the numbers of judgeships. It may be that the parties are less concerned with the welfare of the judges than with multiplying and intensifying the attractions they can hold out to prospective followers, but whatever their motivations, the effect is to better the rewards, lighten the burdens, and augment the influence of judges.

These bonds between parties and the judicial system arising from the search for representativeness engendered a familiar reaction: the quest for political neutrality and technical competence. Judicial terms of office were lengthened to make judges more independent of party influences. Although only two states followed the federal example and conferred life terms on some of their justices, almost all the other states introduced long tenure for both elected and appointed judges, Pennsylvania lengthening to 21 years the term for members of its supreme court. Judges' salaries are often guaranteed against reduction during their tenure, and elaborate safeguards against arbitrary removal have been erected. Most states require at least admission to the bar as a prerequisite to elevation to any but the most minor places on the bench, and some prescribe several years of experience. In some instances civic reformers have induced party leaders and chief executives with powers of judicial appointment to submit to bar associations for approval the names of their proposed candidates for judicial vacancies, and have even persuaded party leaders (who were not entirely averse to the idea) not to run opposing candidates against incumbent judges who have performed satisfactorily.

These innovations are about as far as advocates of nonpartisan competence have gone in this field. No one has yet suggested that the selection of judges be turned over to a body analogous to a civil-service commission, with tests to determine the fitness of candidates for the bench. Judges make too many important policy decisions for people readily to insulate them completely from the effects of representative institutions. California, Missouri, and Alaska have, however, moved in this direction. In the first state the governor's appointments must be approved by a commission on qualifications consisting of three *ex officio* members, while in the latter two the governors' discretion is restricted to lists of names prepared by commissions of lawyers and laymen. Missouri also employs nonpartisan elections for judges (i.e., elections in which no party labels appear on the ballots).[23] In the light of all the forces that bind judges and parties together, one may wonder whether to take literally the observation of the chief justice of Missouri that this plan "has taken the courts out of politics." But the objectives and the slogan are familiar; the architects of government want more than representativeness and its consequences.

Increasingly, voices are heard urging appointment by chief executives rather than election as a mode of judicial selection. Many specialists in judicial administration who favor this change do so less because they want to strengthen the executives than because they hope this move will raise the competence of the men elevated to the bench. In the broad and highly visible arena of executive action, civic groups, reform groups, bar associations, law school officers, and others can often exert their demands as effectively as party leaders can press *their* claims. Nominations for elective office other than the highest executive posts are often made in relative obscurity by the inner circles of the regular party organizations, and these other interests find it difficult to apply much leverage there. The motives of those who have come to prefer appointment of judges to election of judges, however, does not alter the results such a shift would have. Beyond any question it would magnify the ability of the executive to furnish his own brand of leadership in government. So even on the judicial side, there are signs of growing receptivity to the values that have shaped the other branches of government during the twentieth century. This movement, though, is still in its initial stages; on balance, our judicial system still represents primarily a compromise between representativeness and neutral competence.

[23] Phillips, *State and Local Government in America*, pp. 238–240; Anderson, Penniman, and Weidner, *op. cit.*, p. 290.

The Architecture of State and Local Governments

New tests of the ingenuity of the designers of governmental machinery, of their capacity to adjust organization and procedure to reflect the three values that have loomed so large in the architecture of state and local governments, are already visible on the horizon. The population of the United States has undergone an enormous natural increase—almost 3 million net a year for more than a decade. Yet during the same period the farm populace has been decreasing, our large cities have not kept pace with the national increase, and some cities have even *lost* people during this interval. Where, then, has the rise occurred? The answer is obvious: in the environs of the cities. Almost two-thirds of the people in this country live in 174 metropolitan areas; that is to say, cities of 50,000 and the surrounding territories socially and economically integrated with them. In these surrounding regions population figures have soared.

These changes have taxed existing facilities to the limit. Railroads have been staggered by the new loads, and service worsens even though fares climb rapidly. Commuters thereupon turn to the highways, cutting down railroad revenues, so rates climb still higher and still more people then take to their automobiles. Overloaded highways produce massive traffic jams, and the costs of additional roads skyrocket. Meanwhile, the suburbs have had to build school systems almost overnight, find and deliver water, put in sewer systems (yet avoid contaminating neighboring communities), shift from volunteer to professional firefighting services, expand police forces, build parks and other recreational facilities, and perform all these functions with a tax base built largely on private homeowners. The transfer of population induces developers to put up huge shopping centers in outlying areas, centers created for the automobile age, and downtown stores in the middle of the core cities now feel the competition. Declining business, plus deterioration of older structures, prevent core-city tax *bases* from keeping pace with inflation, and increasing tax *rates* drive more people to the suburbs. The plans of one community are nullified by the actions of another. One attracts industry to improve sources of revenue, and adjacent ones endure the costs of heavier traffic, greater congestion, and dirtier (and perhaps more malodorous) air without sharing in the added income. And communities vying with one another for industry sometimes make disastrous tax and other concessions to firms in order to entice them. The swift demographic and economic transformation of the cities and their surroundings has produced very real problems.

The people caught up in this whirl of events, with its frustrations, abrasions, irritations, aggravations, confusions, and disappointments grumble and complain and put up with them, although some who fled to the

24 Cf., Robert C. Wood, *Suburbia* (Boston: Houghton Mifflin, 1959), Chapter 3; Lewis Mumford, *The City in History* (New York: Harcourt, Brace and World, 1961), Chapters 16, 17. See also, Phillips, *Municipal Government and Administration in America*, Chapter VI, for a more traditional summation of the political science doctrine on metropolitan areas. For an unusually perceptive analysis of a single such area—the New York metropolitan region—see Robert C. Wood, *1400 Governments* (Cambridge: Harvard University Press, 1961).

suburbs in search of bucolic delights have fled back to the cities again. Government officials in these regions have coped with the challenges on an *ad hoc* basis, meeting each emergency in turn and reaching policy decisions in a piecemeal fashion. And somehow things go along without bogging down—just barely avoiding collapse, according to some observers, but getting on, at any rate.

To many students of government, however, the situation seems chaotic, inefficient, costly, and intolerable. Worse, they fear what might happen if present trends continue and there is no planned and concerted response to them. Even before the turn of the century there were reformers who saw what was coming and proposed that metropolitan governmental machinery be revised to prepare for the changes. During the thirties and forties their ranks swelled a little and their voices grew louder, but they still attracted little attention. After World War II, as the problems grew more acute and pressing, things changed. Federal urban renewal programs, research sponsored by foundations, the growing concern of civic and business groups, and the investigation of metropolitan problems by mass media of communication all combined to lend the reformers more resources, sympathy, and outlets to the public than they had ever before enjoyed. The volume of reports and studies mushroomed, and at last were followed by action. The vanguard of what promises to be a new wave of governmental reorganization in urban areas has arrived.

Although there will be many variations, the main theme of reorganization is already apparent. Some kind of region-wide coordinating machinery in metropolitan areas will be established. Existing communities, their governments, and their political party leaders are too strongly entrenched, and too powerful in the state legislatures which would have to approve these changes, to permit themselves to be abolished and incorporated into new super-cities, each extending over an entire metropolitan region. The arrangements will therefore have to accommodate these factors, yet still furnish the central direction so many commentators believe is essential. The classic model under such circumstances is the federal government itself, to which the states gave only such powers as they thought necessary to sustain the whole system, reserving all the others to themselves. There is every reason to suspect this is the way the new metropolitan units of government will get their start.

Exactly what the forms will be is hard to say. Where the greater part of the region lies within county boundaries, as most of them do, chances are the county governments will be modernized and utilized for this purpose. Dade County, Florida (which contains Miami) is an example, while Westchester and Nassau Counties in New York and Los Angeles County in California in somewhat different ways have made strides of this kind. A similar plan for St. Louis failed of adoption but is apt to be pressed again in the future. Where a region transcends county lines, some sort of regional council representing all or most of the communities in the area will probably be set up. Metropolitan Toronto is the outstanding example here, for the council for this area has considerable authority and some taxing power. In the New York metropolitan region an embryo council for New York City and 17 nearby counties in New York State, New Jersey, and Connecticut, without power and without statutory base, is still only

The Architecture of State and Local Governments

a straw in the wind. Until some generally acceptable format is devised, temporary expedients—agreements between neighboring communities, unifunctional special districts, and others—will be adopted to alleviate particular sorts of distress. In the end, though, some kind of federal plan will undoubtedly become the norm.

There is no evidence on which to predict what the division of functions between the metropolitan government and the constituent communities will be. Indeed, in the beginning, the metropolitan unit that reaches for independent financial authority is likely to encounter suspicious and hostile resistance. In many regions the first endeavors may well resemble the Articles of Confederation rather than the Constitution. If so, will the relations between the center and the component units follow the same course as relations between Washington and the states? Here is a test and a challenge for political theory!

Reformers urging reorganization have been baffled and upset by the lack of response in the communities they seek to aid; they express dismay over the lack of metropolitan leadership. Moreover, they have encountered criticism, not merely from those with a stake in the status quo, but from the fringe groups on the extreme right, who regard proposals for metropolitan government (as they seem to regard all change) as a communist plot, and from those on the other side of the fence who suspect the move to extend the borders of urban governments is a way of "containing" the growing political strength of Negroes and other nonwhites in the core cities. Certainly the plan will meet opposition from many groups and indifference on the part of most of the people affected.[25] Reform movements, however, are almost always the work of small, dedicated, well-financed, persistent minorities who have connections in high places and media for airing their views. Indeed, the creation in 1898 of the Greater City of New York out of the old New York City (Manhattan and parts of The Bronx), the city of Brooklyn, and the smaller municipalities and settlements in the environs, was in many respects the work of one indefatigable and dauntless man, Andrew Haswell Green. There may be some reason to wonder whether the recommended remedy will cure all the alleged ills, but there is also good reason to conclude it will eventually be tried in any event.

From all we have seen, the architects of the new governmental form will have to reconcile in their design the competing claims of representativeness, neutral competence, and executive leadership. Perhaps they will start with something of an advantage over their predecessors in earlier generations, for they will have before them the lessons of excessive stress on any of these values and of neglect of any of them. On the other hand, perhaps there is no way to balance the three values at the very start. It will be interesting to see how they solve these problems.

A Matter of Choice

We opened this chapter with the remark that men build their governments the way they build houses. Perhaps it would have been more accurate to have said the way they build cathedrals. For houses are built in

25 Cf., Wood, *1400 Governments*, Chapter 5.

weeks or months or at most in years, but governments and cathedrals take generations and even centuries to construct. In a great cathedral it is sometimes possible to detect changes in style and fashion that occurred during the course of construction, each shift of taste leaving its mark on the final edifice. In the same way, changes in political styles, preferences, and values register themselves over time on governmental institutions. This phenomenon is particularly evident in the government and politics of states and localities in the United States. Originally the products of the political folkways and mores of one era's designers, they have been modified, revamped, rebuilt, expanded, redirected, added to, rejected, reinstated, suppressed, and partially abandoned by every subsequent set of architects. What is prized at one time may be derided at another; what is neglected in one period may (perhaps for that very reason) become the central concern of the next. Thus every generation leaves its deposit of structures and procedures on the institutions it inherits. As one might expect, the outcome is rather rambling, inconsistent, and lacking in coherence and symmetry. It is not efficient in an engineering sense.

But Americans cleave to values other than engineering efficiency in constructing their governmental institutions. Specifically, representativeness, nonpartisan competence, and executive leadership have evidently been more highly prized than neatness, order, continuity, calculated rationality, and smoothness of operation. The United States is a young nation, but all three of these values have left their impress in its short life. Where the burdens and responsibilities of governments have been heaviest, the transition from emphasis on one value to emphasis on another has been most rapid, which explains why the residues of all three persist in states and in cities. Where the pace of life or the scope of governmental activity has been limited, as in the non-urban areas and in most of the narrowly specific special districts, new values have not forced changes in governmental design. Where a function is exceptionally specialized and deliberately allocated to a category of its own, as is the judicial function, executive leadership may be suppressed rather than sought the way the other two values are. Where governmental organization is in flux because of highly fluid social and economic conditions, as in metropolitan regions, we may anticipate a frantic search for ways of maximizing all three values in the instruments being forged. In the future, governmental architecture may come to reflect values altogether unforeseen right now.

Does what we have just said mean that governmental organization and procedure in states and localities are products of nothing more than fads and fancies of the moment? Do Americans change their political structures and practices merely out of restlessness and a propensity to tinker with machinery? Far from it! Implicit in the search for new values and in the accompanying reconstruction of government is a contest for very sizable rewards imbedded in virtually all public decisions. To the nature of these rewards, how they are distributed, the seekers after them, and the strategies of the seekers we turn in the next chapters.

The Architecture of State and Local Governments

Everyone's
in Politics

CHAPTER THREE

In discussing the "architects" and "designers"
of governmental structure, we have as a matter of convenience
talked as though there were a separate group who, alone
among all persons who take part in politics, are concerned with developing
proposals of this kind and guiding them from conception to adoption.
Actually, there is no such distinct, specialized group, although
there are some students of and participants
in government who consistently give this aspect of our
political life more attention and more systematic

65

thought than others. But the character of all our political institutions and processes is molded by all those who play a role in making governmental decisions of all kinds. And when you get right down to it, practically everyone in each of our political communities, from nation to hamlet, assumes a role of this kind in some way and at some time. In a broad sense, everyone's in politics.

Of course, this statement implies a much broader conception of the scope of politics than many people subscribe to in ordinary discourse. Usually, when people talk of politics, they mean the processes by which leading positions in parties are filled, and by which party leaders distribute nominations, appointments, and special favors. These considerations, however, although important, are only a part of what we refer to here when we use the term. Throughout our analysis, "politics" will include all the decisions and actions of government officials and employees, party leaders and members, voters, *and all the methods and strategies employed by these people and any other individuals and groups to influence such actions and decisions.* Thus an effort by a civic group to block a party nomination, an attempt by a bar association to induce an executive to appoint a candidate the association supports, an endeavor to reorganize a government or a branch of the government or a public department or agency, the circulation of a petition to improve conditions in a school, the barricading of a street by mothers demanding traffic signals be set up, the bribing of a building inspector to overlook a technically forbidden electrical installation, and the "fixing" of a traffic ticket—all represent participation in politics. In fact, even people who have never done any of these things or anything similar to them, who may never even have *voted,* influence political decisions, for other participants in the political process calculate their own strategies by estimating who is likely to be active and who unconcerned and apathetic. The nonparticipants thus encourage some participants and discourage others. Defined in this way, politics touches everybody.

Obviously, you cannot get very far with such an inclusive definition by itself; a definition that excludes nothing is useless. But to begin by recognizing that politics is not the preserve of a few professional party and government officials is to take a long step toward a deeper understanding of the governmental process.

The Stakes and Prizes of Political Action[1]

Perhaps the easiest way to make this point is to examine the stakes and prizes people win when they resort to political action. It is hardly possible in a study of this kind to delve into all the complex and hidden psychological forces driving each individual, but it is within our grasp to identify and categorize the kinds of objectives to which participants address themselves and the types of rewards they actually obtain, whatever obscure and intricate factors may motivate them.

In these terms office itself, whether elective or appointive, is palpably one of the main ones. Admittedly, office is often merely a means to other

---

[1] This section is adapted from Wallace S. Sayre and Herbert Kaufman, *Governing New York City* (New York: Russell Sage Foundation, 1960), Chapter II.

Everyone's in Politics

prizes—money, prestige, control of policy, or the like. But it is sometimes an end in itself, and is sought by men who already possess practically all the rewards public office can bestow save office itself. It is not a stake for which only would-be occupants strive, however. Officeholders' sponsors and allies, the interests served and regulated, the claimants who seek favorable appointments or decisions, colleagues and superiors and subordinates, and many other groups also focus their energies on influencing how vacancies in public offices and employment are filled. No nomination, no election, no appointment is a purely private affair of the lucky winner. Many persons will have their eyes on him and on the process by which he was chosen, and many will share in his triumph or his disappointment.

Another type of political stake is governmental service,[2] which includes both what is done *for* people and what is done *to* them for the benefit of others. Building a highway, for instance, makes life easier for persons who use it, but inconveniences those who are displaced to make way for it; and regulating air pollution is a burden to industries that must install smoke-abatement equipment, but is a blessing to those relieved of airborne irritants. A high percentage of political action is directed toward influencing governmental decisions about the kinds of service to render and the kinds of regulations to impose, and each such decision is certain to elicit ardent support and vigorous opposition.

Many of the things state and local governments do would otherwise have to be obtained in the marketplace; indeed, many public services have private counterparts and supplements. There are private and parochial schools and universities, private police and detective agencies, volunteer fire departments, voluntary health organizations, private charities, commercial refuse removal firms, and numerous other parallels to public functions that clients and customers may turn to, and to which *all* who wanted those services would be compelled to go if there were no governmental programs in these fields. By the same token, there are publicly owned and operated electric utilities, transportation facilities, water works, liquor stores, hospitals, housing developments, and other enterprises more commonly regarded as private in our society. There are also many functions that no private undertaking could effectively perform—law enforcement, judicial administration, and public health regulation come readily to mind as illustrations—and many programs governments could embark upon, but do not (such as medical and hospital insurance). In other words, prevailing divisions between public and private activity constitute patterns of political settlement among citizens who demand particular services and citizens who resist them. Few settlements are permanent; the lines are constantly under pressure, and hence continually redrawn.

Economic stakes compose a third category. The stakes of governmental service overlap with economic stakes in important respects, for the costs of public service are usually spread over the entire community (al-

---

[2] For a brief catalogue of state and local governmental services, see John M. Swarthout and Ernest R. Bartley, *Principles and Problems of State and Local Government* (New York: Oxford University Press, 1958), Chapter X. See also, William Anderson and Edward W. Weidner, *American City Government*, rev. ed. (New York: Holt, 1950), pp. 71–85, and the works cited therein at p. 100; W. Brooke Graves, *American State Government* 4th ed. (Boston: D. C. Heath and Co., 1953), Chapter 12.

Everyone's in Politics

Table 13 PUBLIC EMPLOYMENT AND PAYROLLS, by Functions and Levels of Government, October, 1961

Functions	Employees					October Payroll				
	Total	Federal (civilian)[a]	State and Local			Total	Federal (civilian)[b]	State and Local		
			Total	State	Local			Total	State	Local
	Number (in thousands)					Amount (in millions of dollars)				
Total	9,100	2,484	6,616	1,627	4,990	3,633.5	1,213.6	2,419.9	587.2	1,832.7
National defense and international relations	1,070	1,070	—	—	—	536.3	536.3	—	—	—
Postal service	580	580	—	—	—	252.6	252.6	—	—	—
Education	3,062	12	3,050	520	2,530	1,210.8	6.2	1,204.6	178.0	1,026.6
Highways	545	5	540	256	284	194.2	3.0	191.2	98.4	92.8
Health and hospitals	879	177	702	346	356	291.2	74.3	216.9	112.8	104.0
Police protection	367	22	345	34	311	146.9	13.9	133.0	15.1	117.9
Natural resources	334	189	145	113	32	149.3	98.5	50.8	41.2	9.6
Financial administration	292	80	212	74	138	112.7	44.7	68.0	29.5	38.5
General control	265	32	233	23	210	90.6	19.2	71.4	12.2	59.3
All other	1,706	317	1,389	259	1,130	648.9	164.9	484.0	99.9	384.1
Total (% distribution)	100.0	100.0	100.0	100.0	100.0	100.0	100.0	100.0	100.0	100.0
National defense and international relations	11.8	43.1	—	—	—	14.8	44.2	—	—	—
Postal service	6.4	23.3	—	—	—	7.0	20.8	—	—	—
Education	33.6	0.5	46.1	32.0	50.7	33.3	0.5	49.8	30.3	56.0
Highways	6.0	0.2	8.2	15.7	5.7	5.3	0.2	7.9	16.8	5.1
Health and hospitals	9.7	7.1	10.6	21.3	7.1	8.0	6.1	9.0	19.2	5.7
Police protection	4.0	0.9	5.2	2.1	6.2	4.0	1.1	5.5	2.6	6.4
Natural resources	3.7	7.6	2.2	6.9	0.6	4.1	8.1	2.1	7.0	0.5
Financial administration	3.2	3.2	3.2	4.5	2.8	3.1	3.7	2.8	5.0	2.1
General control	2.9	1.3	3.5	1.4	4.2	2.5	1.6	3.0	2.1	3.2
All other	18.7	12.8	21.0	15.9	22.6	17.9	13.6	20.0	17.0	21.0

[a] Comprises all federal civilian employees, including those outside United States as well as 36 thousand employees of the National Guard paid directly from the federal Treasury.

[b] Includes $16 million for employees of the National Guard.

Note: Statistics for local governments are subject to sampling variations. Because of rounding, detail may not add to total.

Source: U.S. Bureau of the Census. State Distribution of Public Employment in 1961 (April 27, 1962), p. 7.

though they *may* be levied on users, as in the case of tolls and fees and special assessments for improvements, for example), in which case the immediate beneficiaries may carry less of a financial load than they would if they were compelled to buy the service in the market. Over and above this consideration, however, governmental actions have far-reaching economic consequences. For, as we have seen, state and local governments disburse immense sums of money. They are therefore obliged to raise large amounts of money, and they make a host of other decisions that improve the economic position of some people and handicap others.

With regard to public spending,[3] consider governments' roles as employers (Tables 13 and 14). Should they yield to the requests of public employees for pay increases and fringe benefits, or should they heed instead the advocates of economy? Either group might punish governmental leaders at the polls. Think of all the things government agencies buy, from power shovels and fire trucks to electric light bulbs and kitchen matches; should they favor local businessmen even if they must pay a little more, or should they take their business out of the community or out of the state if they can save a few hundred dollars? And who among the local vendors should get the account? Contemplate the volume of construction in public buildings, public roads, and other public works. Should contracts be confined only to residents of the area being served, or opened to outside bidding? Should the work be divided up, or should one bidder take it all and thereby acquire the power that goes with subcontracting? Reflect on the millions spent on public welfare; should assistance be given to newcomers to a community, or restricted only to persons who have resided there for a time? Under what conditions should it be withheld? What kinds of programs and what kinds of benefits should be provided? These are but a few of the questions that move people to political action.

Many citizens who display comparative indifference to decisions about office, service, and spending as such will often spring to life on a different set of issues: public revenues (Tables 15, 16, 17, 18). Some people can be counted on to fight any increase in any kind of taxation or borrowing. Most people are aroused principally by taxes that fall on them. As things have worked out over time, the federal government has pre-empted the income tax, both corporate and personal, which is the most lucrative source of revenue in the country, and which does not lend itself to administration on less than a national basis if the rates are to be at all substantial. States have turned heavily to excise and sales taxes, both general and special (e.g., gasoline, cigarettes, and liquor). Localities still depend heavily on real property taxes, although income from publicly owned and operated utilities, from sales taxes, and even from income taxes have come to play an ever larger part in their financing. Most special districts (but not school districts, which have powers of taxation) exist on the tolls, charges, and rents they levy for the use of their facilities. But all state and local governments use all forms of taxation to some extent. And each new adoption, each change in the going configuration, invariably provokes storms of controversy even in quarters ordinarily quiescent about government.

For what is to be decided here is who picks up the check, who pays

---

[3] See Tables 4 to 9, inclusive.   **69**

Table 14   EMPLOYMENT AND PAYROLLS OF STATE AND LOCAL GOVERNMENTS, by Functions, October, 1961

Function	All employees (full-time and part-time) (in thousands)			Full-time equivalent employment (in thousands)			Monthly payroll (in millions of dollars)			Average monthly earnings of full-time employees
	Total	State	Local	Total	State	Local	Total	State	Local	
All functions	6,616	1,627	4,990	5,845	1,437	4,408	2,419.9	587.2	1,832.7	$415
Education	3,050	520	2,530	2,652	369	2,283	1,204.6	178.0	1,026.6	458
Local schools	2,491	11	2,480	2,259	10	2,249	1,012.2	4.8	1,007.4	453
Instructional personnel	1,686	9	1,677	1,600	8	1,592	818.1	4.1	814.0	511
Other	805	2	803	658	2	656	194.1	0.7	193.4	296
Institutions of higher education	527	477	50	364	330	34	179.9	160.7	19.2	502
Instructional personnel	177	148	29	142	121	21	99.6	85.3	14.3	697
Other	350	329	21	222	209	13	80.3	75.4	4.9	366
Other education	32	32	—	29	29	—	12.5	12.5	—	426
Functions other than education	3,566	1,106	2,460	3,193	1,068	2,125	1,215.3	409.2	806.1	380
Highways	540	256	284	514	252	262	191.2	98.4	92.8	372
Public welfare	131	49	82	125	47	78	44.6	17.2	27.4	356
Hospitals	619	317	302	601	312	289	185.6	100.9	84.8	309
Health	82	28	54	77	28	49	31.2	12.0	19.3	408
Police protection	345	34	311	310	34	276	133.0	15.1	117.9	429
Local fire protection	221	—	221	160	—	160	74.1	—	74.1	463
Sewerage	52	—	52	48	—	48	19.0	—	19.0	392
Sanitation other than sewerage	110	—	110	106	—	106	37.9	—	37.9	358
Local parks and recreation	108	—	108	90	—	90	32.4	—	32.4	357
Natural resources	145	113	32	126	100	26	50.8	41.2	9.6	405
Housing and urban renewal	33	—	33	32	—	32	12.7	—	12.7	399
Airports	11	—	11	10	—	10	4.0	—	4.0	412
Water transport and terminals	9	—	9	8	—	8	3.8	—	3.8	492
Correction	93	59	34	91	58	33	36.2	22.3	13.9	398
Local libraries	55	—	55	42	—	42	13.2	—	13.2	318
Financial administration	212	74	138	177	73	104	68.0	29.5	38.5	386
General control	233	23	210	175	21	154	71.4	12.2	59.3	410
Local utilities:										
Water supply	108	—	108	100	—	100	38.5	—	38.5	386
Electric power	58	—	58	56	—	56	25.7	—	25.7	457
Transit	71	—	71	71	—	71	30.3	—	30.3	429
Gas supply	6	—	6	6	—	6	2.2	—	2.2	368
Other and unallocable	324	153	171	269	144	125	109.6	60.6	49.0	405

Note: Statistics for local governments are subject to sampling variation. Because of rounding, detail may not add to total.

Source: U.S. Bur...

Table 15 GENERAL REVENUES (In millions of dollars) of Governments from Their Own Sources,[a] by Sources and by Levels of Government, 1960

	All Governments	Federal	State and Local Total	State	Local
General revenue from own sources	131,557	88,027	43,530	20,618	22,912
Taxes	113,120	77,003	36,117	18,036	18,081
Property	16,405	—	16,405	607	15,798
Individual income	43,178	40,715	2,463	2,209	254
Corporation income	22,674	21,494	1,180	1,180	b—
Sales and gross receipts	24,452	12,603	11,849	10,510	1,339
Customs duties	1,105	1,105	—	—	—
General sales and gross receipts	5,177	—	5,177	4,302	875
Selective sales and gross receipts	18,170	11,498	6,672	6,208	464
Motor fuel	5,352	1,984	3,368	3,335	33
Alcoholic beverages	3,779	3,106	673	650	23
Tobacco products	2,915	1,927	988	923	65
Public utilities	1,627	994	633	365	268
Other	4,498	3,487	1,011	935	76
Motor vehicle and operators licenses	1,700	—	1,700	1,573	127
Death and gift	2,026	1,606	420	420	c—
All other	2,685	585	2,100	1,535	565
Charges and miscellaneous general revenue	18,438	11,024	7,414	2,583	4,831
Current charges	13,390	8,071	5,319	1,783	3,536
National defense and international relations	761	761	—	—	—
Postal service	3,260	3,260	—	—	—
Education	1,802	6	1,796	850	946
School lunch sales	688	—	688	—	688
Other	1,114	6	1,108	850	258
Highways	569	1	568	382	186
Natural resources	3,510	3,331	179	102	77
Hospitals	911	28	883	233	650
Sewers and sewage disposal	318	—	318	—	318
Other sanitation	104	—	104	—	104
Local parks and recreation	105	—	105	—	105
Housing	534	195	339	3	336
Air transportation	150	3	147	7	140
Water transport and terminals	247	104	143	39	104
Other	1,119	382	737	167	570
Special assessments	369	—	369	—	369
Sale of property	289	48	241	27	214
Interest earnings	1,462	818	644	324	320
Other miscellaneous general revenue	2,927	2,087	840	449	391

[a] Excludes revenues from utilities, liquor stores, insurance trusts (such as unemployment compensation, employee retirement, etc.), and intergovernmental revenues. (For these figures, see Tables 16 and 17.)

[b] Minor amount included in individual income tax figure.

[c] Minor amount included in "All other taxes."

Source: U.S. Bureau of the Census, *Governmental Finances in 1960* (September 19, 1961), p. 16.

Everyone's in Politics

Table 16

Table 16   OTHER THAN GENERAL REVENUES OF GOVERNMENTS (in millions of dollars)
by Sources and by Levels of Government, 1960

	All Governments	Federal	State and Local		
			Both	State	Local
Intergovernmental revenue	—[a]	—	6,974	6,745	9,953
From federal government	—[a]	—	6,974	6,382	592
From states	—[a]	—	—[a]	—	9,361
From local governments	—[a]	—	—[a]	363	—[a]
Utility revenue[b]	3,613	—	3,613	—	3,613
Liquor stores revenue	1,264	—	1,264	1,128	136
Insurance trust revenue[c]	17,608	12,712	4,896	4,347	549

[a] Duplicative transactions between levels of government are excluded in arriving at aggregates. See Note b, Table 17.
[b] Water supply, electric power, transit, gas supply systems.
[c] Unemployment compensation; employee retirement; old age, survivors, and disability insurance; veterans life insurance; railroad retirement.
Source: U.S. Bureau of the Census, *Governmental Revenues in 1960* (September 19, 1961), pp. 16, 21, 22.

the bill. If a government relies on a general sales tax, the impact of the tax tends to fall most heavily on low-income groups, for most of their money is spent on consumer items; and merchants too complain because higher sales taxes are often followed by a decline in purchasing. On the other hand, property owners protest the imposition of additional burdens on them. But middle- and upper-income groups resist progressive income taxes, and communities that resort to these devices fear they will drive population, commerce, and industry to more hospitable locations. If offi-

Table 17   TOTAL REVENUES (in millions of dollars), all Governments,
all Sources, by Levels of Government, 1960

	All Governments	Federal	State and Local		
			Both	State	Local
General revenue from own sources	131,557	88,027	43,530	20,618	22,912
Utility revenue	3,613	—	3,613	—	3,613
Liquor stores revenue	1,264	—	1,264	1,128	136
Insurance trust revenue	17,608	12,712	4,896	4,347	549
Total, own sources	154,041[c]	100,739	53,302[c]	26,093	27,209[c]
Intergovernmental revenue[b]	—[a]	—	6,974	6,745	9,953
Federal government	—[a]	—	6,974	6,382	592
States	—[a]	—	—[a]	—	9,361
Local governments	—[a]	—	—[a]	363	—[a]

[a] Duplicative transactions excluded from aggregates.
[b] Revenues of the Federal government include funds eventually granted to state and local governments. State grants to local governments come partly from these Federal grants, partly from the states' own sources. Consequently, if intergovernmental revenues were counted each time and intergovernmental transfers were made, they would be counted more than once and therefore are not added into the totals for governmental revenues.
[c] Because of rounding, detail does not add to totals.
Source: U.S. Bureau of the Census, *Governmental Revenues in 1960* (September 19, 1961), p. 16.

Everyone's in Politics

Table 18 SELECTED ITEMS OF LOCAL GOVERNMENT FINANCES (In billions of dollars)
by Type of Government, 1960

	All local governments	Counties	Munici- palities	Town- ships	School districts	Special districts
All general revenue from own sources	22.9	4.3	9.3	1.1	7.0	1.2
Tax revenue	18.1	3.4	7.1	1.0	6.1	0.5
Property tax	15.8	3.2	5.2	0.9	6.0	0.5
Other taxes	2.3	0.3	1.9	—ᵃ	0.1	—
Charges and miscellane- ous general revenue	4.8	0.8	2.2	0.1	0.9	0.8
Direct general expenditure	33.9	6.6	11.7	1.3	12.6	1.7
Education	15.2	0.6	1.8	0.4	12.3	0.1
Highways	3.4	1.4	1.6	0.3	—	0.1
Public welfare	2.2	1.5	0.6	0.1	—	—
Health and hospitals	1.9	0.9	0.8	—ᵃ	—	0.2
All other	11.2	2.2	7.0	0.5	0.4	1.1
Debt outstanding, total	51.4	5.1	23.2	1.1	12.1	9.9
Long-term	48.7	5.0	21.9	1.0	11.8	9.0
Full faith and credit	32.7	4.0	14.5	1.0	11.8	1.4
Nonguaranteed	15.9	0.9	7.4	—ᵃ	—	7.6
Cash and security holdings, total	22.1	2.8	12.5	0.6	3.9	2.3
Cash and deposits	8.7	2.0	3.3	0.5	2.2	0.7
Securities	13.4	0.8	9.2	0.1	1.7	1.6

ᵃ Less than $50 million.

Note: Because of rounding, detail may not add to totals. These data are estimates subject to sampling variations.

Source: U.S. Bureau of the Census, Governmental Finances in 1960 (September 19, 1961), p. 23.

cials turn in desperation to special sales taxes, the industries affected, and all the purveyors of the products, rise up in arms—sometimes to fight the tax, as the oil companies have attacked taxation of gasoline, sometimes to insist the revenues be allocated exclusively to the interests taxed, as the automobile associations have battled against the application of gasoline tax revenues to any function but road-building and upkeep. Governments

Table 19   STATE AND LOCAL GOVERNMENTAL DEBT AND DEBT CHARGES (In millions of dollars), 1960

	Debt Outstanding	Interest on Debt
States	18,543	536
Local governments	51,412	1,134
Total	69,945	1,670

Source: U.S. Bureau of the Census, Governmental Finances in 1960 (September 19, 1961), pp. 4, 22.

can borrow money, but if they issue bonds to pay for recurrent expenses they will soon be in debt over their heads; in addition, borrowing builds up interest charges to levels beyond the capacity of the governments to bear (Tables 3 and 19). Anyway, banks and individual investors who already hold bonds exert pressure to prevent reckless borrowing because this jeopardizes their own investments. On the other hand, if a state or locality tries to pay for everything out of current income, they saddle the current generation with the costs of facilities that future generations will benefit from. These dilemmas sometimes compel governments to levy "nuisance" taxes on any stream of commerce that promises to produce even a small return, but New York City discovered that these levies, too, can generate passionate political reactions. When the city placed a ten-cent tax on taxi rides, the drivers, who claimed passengers simply reduced the size of their tips by the amount of the tax, organized a mass taxi caravan to the state capital in protest. The tax was repealed the next year.

In short, every group strives to transfer the costs of public services from themselves to someone else. When revenue measures are under consideration, they mobilize and speak out vigorously; when measures are adopted, the groups affected make their displeasure known; when elections come around, they use their influence to penalize parties and officials they hold responsible. Each of the participants tends to think of his antagonists as "playing politics" while they themselves are not. To the disinterested observer, it is quite clear that all are in politics very deeply, even if only once in a while (and perhaps this is as it should be in a healthy democratic polity).

Spending and taxing and borrowing and service policies obviously affect the economic position of all groups in a governmental jurisdiction, but hardly more so than—indeed, perhaps not as much as—still another category of governmental actions: various forms of public regulation of economic activity.[4] Regulation of rates and other aspects of business is one of these forms. Most states have instituted some type of controls on railroads, trucks, buses, utilities, banks, insurance companies, and other businesses; the decisions to impose controls, and then each of the regulatory decisions reached under the general laws, ordinarily stimulate a torrent of pressures and counterpressures. Customers (and this includes large companies and associations of companies as well as individuals) favor governmental supervision; the interests regulated oppose it. When the regulated interests seek permission to raise rates and charges, customers fight to hold them down. If a corporation rendering a service tries to curtail the volume or quality of service, their customers apply political leverage to prevent them from doing so. City banks hoping to open branches in neighboring areas find local banks mobilized to stop the invasion. Almost invariably, everything connected with economic regulation incites some people to action in the governmental arena.

Setting standards of performance is another form of regulation that affects returns on private investments. The stricter the building codes, for example, the higher the cost of houses (but the better off the skilled laborers who construct them). Stringent limitations on the butterfat content of milk, the amount of water in meat, or the risks to which workers

[4] Swarthout and Bartley, *op. cit.*, Chapter XI.

may be subjected affect directly the operating costs and maybe even the profits of entrepreneurs. Laws forbidding stores to operate on Sundays cut into their potential volume of business. As a result, every time standards are set or changed, the people concerned are roused, and public officials quickly learn that the circle of interested groups is much wider than one might intuitively expect, and that the pressure to modify standards never abates.

What is more, the *enforcement* of standards is a center of pressure, too. Sometimes the interests affected will argue for a favorable interpretation of a general regulation—claiming exemption from part of its provisions, say. Sometimes they will try, by legitimate or by illicit means, to sway the judgment of an inspector regarding their adherence to adopted standards. In general, efforts to influence enforcement decisions tend to be less visible and organized than the efforts connected with adoption or adjustment of standards, but it is by no means unusual for a substantial segment of the business community to act in concert on matters of enforcement.

Another kind of governmental decision from which widespread economic consequences ensue is the granting of licenses and franchises. The latter usually confer a monopoly on the recipient, but even licenses may be used to limit the number of competitors in a given field of activity. Inevitably, rivalries for these advantages grow intense, and maneuvers to acquire them are carefully calculated and strenuously conducted. It is no wonder that some of the most glaring scandals in American government have been linked to the quest for these forms of economic preferment.

Finally, state and local governments make decisions about the uses to which land may be put, and these decisions vitally affect the economic status of a wide variety of people and enterprises. A locality maintaining a one-acre minimum for the construction of houses, for instance, may thus succeed in excluding developers (who require greater density in order to make their investments pay), and thereby debar from entry potential residents unable to afford or obtain the larger tracts. On the other hand, a major highway cutting through a residential section may depreciate property values because of the noise and odors the construction spawns. A thruway will divert traffic and trade from businesses on older roads. An area open to business development in a residential neighborhood may bring rich returns to the businessmen, but opening *additional* business blocks in such neighborhoods may confront established stores with strong competition. People who want the protection (and lower fire insurance premiums) that come with professional fire departments do not ordinarily like to have the firehouse built next door. So public officials with the responsibilities for making these choices must decide in an atmosphere of tension and controversy. For a citizenry that considers itself nonpolitical, the inhabitants of our states and localities manage to work up impressive pressures.

It would be misleading to conclude this discussion of the stakes of politics with no mention of the non-material prizes which apparently induce many people to enter the political arena. There are those who are ideologically motivated, and struggle—sometimes at great material sacrifice—for policies that for them are fundamental articles of faith. Others, moved by compassion for the suffering and the deprived, devote themselves

75

Everyone's in Politics

to working for programs from which they themselves clearly can derive no personal tangible benefits. Some value moral and religious principles more highly than material reward. There are groups for whom the comparatively open ladders of politics furnish unparalleled opportunities to climb out of the social cellar to which prejudice and entrenched powers otherwise consign them. There are others who are relatively indifferent to state and local issues but are committed to national policies that they think they can advance through their labors in our sub-national governments. Many find in politics a sense of drama, excitement, and fellowship to enrich and enliven their lives. These factors, too, draw people into the world of government and politics, and they are no less significant than the other stakes around which politics revolves.

Actually, the prizes all run together. A victorious candidate not only wins an office but perhaps also an opportunity to promote ideological concepts in which he believes, to open lines of access to governmental decision-makers for his sponsors, and to institute a pattern of services or to pass legislation more congenial to his supporters. By the same token, a change of policy may hurt the chances for one group to win or hold office, or another group to obtain or retain economic advantages for which they had hoped, and a third to further a program in which they were vitally interested. Separating the stakes into distinct categories is an analytical device that underscores the involvement of almost everybody in governmental actions. It indicates why at one time or another practically every citizen will make an active effort to influence a policy decision. But each participant rarely pursues only one end. A decision rarely fulfills only one goal. Things are rarely that simple.

Seekers of the Prizes[5]

Although the range and diversity of the rewards of political action in states and localities involve almost everyone in the governmental process, all persons are not involved to the same extent and in the same way, nor do they all possess identical sources of influence. For this reason it is almost impossible to offer any but the most vacuous generalizations about all of them at once. There are, however, common elements among *sub-sets* of the participants that can be identified and used to classify them for purposes of analysis.

On the basis of the positions they occupy in political systems, there are at least five categories of participants: (1) public officials, both elected and appointed; (2) the leaders of the political parties; (3) the organized public bureaucracies (bureaucracy being used here as a descriptive, not as a critical, term); (4) non-governmental groups of all kinds, including the underworld as well as the spokesmen of legitimate interests, and comprising also the mass media of communication as special kinds of groups; (5) officials and bureaucrats of other governments, including the federal government and the governments of neighboring jurisdictions. Above and beyond all these participants stands the electorate, not a participant in the same sense as the other classes, but in many ways the most influential single voice in the political chorus. Other commentators on

[5] Adapted from Sayre and Kaufman, *op. cit.*, Chapter III.

government may prefer classifications of their own; there is nothing sacred about any set of categories, and the set adopted here is not put forth as superior to or more desirable than its alternatives. It is simply convenient for the kind of analysis attempted in this volume.

None of the categories, incidentally, is monolithic. Officialdom, for instance, comprises legislators, executives, high-rank administrators, and judges of varied constituencies and tenure. Officials are divided according to the specialized functions they perform and the clienteles they serve. They often pursue different goals, establish different loyalties, and generally see the political scene from different points of view. Thus, officials are highly differentiated and even in the same unit of government, rarely act as a single, integrated unit.

Yet they do occupy a unique place in the system. They promulgate formally the official decisions around which so much political action turns; their signatures convert pieces of paper into authoritative documents. Moreover, in formal terms and in governmental theory, and perhaps in fact, they supervise the execution of decisions and often pay the penalties for breakdowns anywhere in the governmental machinery they supervise. They are thus recipients of the system's prizes, distributors of its gifts, and targets of all other participants.

Similarly, parties are like mosaics. As we saw earlier, state organizations are assemblages of county organizations, and county organizations are aggregates of local factions and personal followings. In one-party areas, factionalism is particularly rife, but everywhere the parties are congeries of units that may compete and quarrel with one another almost as frequently as they cooperate.

Like officials, however, they have a distinctive role to play. In two-party areas, they reduce the number of candidates for each office to manageable proportions, keep the system competitive, furnish campaign machinery to win votes for their nominees, and provide voters with some clues about what they are voting for even if the voters are only vaguely familiar with the candidates as individuals. In one-party areas, of course, it is within the mechanism of the party that the *de facto* elections take place, and although they perform few other services, their function is a major and a special one. The central position of parties in nominations and elections makes them similar enough to treat as a class for our purposes despite the diversity they reveal under searching scrutiny.

In speaking of the bureaucrats—i.e., the relatively permanent corps of employees who make up the bulk of governmental personnel—we shall deliberately employ the term "bureaucracies" rather than "bureaucracy" in order to emphasize their diversity.[6] In the earlier part of the nineteenth century, a copy clerk was the archetype of a bureaucrat. By the end of the century, however, this situation had already changed drastically, and today the public services include doctors, lawyers, engineers, accountants, economists, social workers, and teachers, as well as specialized forces like police and firefighters, skilled labor of all kinds, and unskilled laborers in large numbers. Divided by agency, occupation, union or professional association membership, rank, and other characteristics, they almost never act in concert, even on questions in which they share common interests (such

[6] See Tables 13, 14.

as salary, job classification, and working conditions), and often they conflict with one another.

Nevertheless, they are alike in that their day-to-day job performance constitutes the work of governments. They have ideas about what the programs they carry out ought to be, and they are not without the means of influencing both the formulation and execution of policy decisions so that their views are reflected (and sometimes dominant) in what is actually done. Seen from this standpoint, they play similar roles everywhere, even in areas where the range of government services is circumscribed.

Non-governmental groups compose the most variegated category of all:

Some of them have a long history and have had a reputation of power and influence for decades; others are clearly transient and limited in power. They vary in membership from a few score to many thousands. To finance their activities, some nongovernmental groups depend on contributions by a limited number of sponsors, others on donations from the general public, and still others upon dues levied on their members. Their operating budgets range from a few hundred to several hundred thousand dollars a year. The work of smaller, less well-financed groups is generally performed by part-time, volunteer, and amateur workers. Some of the larger, or the more affluent, associations employ permanent, full-time, highly paid professional staffs and provide them with research and secretarial and clerical assistance.

Only a handful . . . are concerned primarily with government. The overwhelming majority are mobilized around other central interests, and active participation in the . . . politicial process is merely one subsidiary phase of much broader sets of interests.[7]

Here are found the labor and business and professional and farm organizations; the veterans associations; the racial, ethnic, national origin, and religious bodies; the health, welfare, and educational societies; neighborhood and other territorial organizations; organizations for the promotion of recreation, of conservation, of hunting and fishing and other sports, of humane treatment for children, of protection of animals; groups concerned with real estate and planning; civic and reform groups; and hosts of *ad hoc* associations, often formed quite spontaneously, to promote or block specific measures under consideration.

In this category, too, we place the communications media, which, by the events and personalities they choose for comprehensive attention and the color they lend to their treatment, exert considerable influence on the selection and behavior of public officers and employees, and on the strategies and effectiveness of other participants as well. In general, the mass media are conscious and deliberate in their political roles, but some of their effects are apparently inadvertent by-products of the dynamics of reporting as a profession and a business, the prejudices and preconceptions of working reporters and editors, and the standards and myths governing "good" reporting and the functions of the mass media in modern society.

All too frequently, groups engaged in activities proscribed by law wield influence in political circles. The most familiar of the underworld organizations are those operating businesses for which there is a large and

[7] Sayre and Kaufman, *op. cit.*, p. 77.

Everyone's in Politics

active clientele willing and able to pay for the services rendered despite the injunctions of law and morality. Organized prostitution, gambling, and narcotics rings are probably the most notorious, but the illegal production and sale of liquor (to avoid taxes or local prohibition) are still practiced. In addition, racketeers have moved in on some business associations and labor unions to use these legitimate forms of organization as means of extorting money and favors from legitimate businessmen and workers. Obviously, illegal groups and operations must avoid saliency, so their methods and interests in the governmental process are limited and specialized. All the same, our picture of politics would be incomplete if we neglected these participants.

Of course, the number and variety of non-governmental groups active in any governmental jurisdiction tend to vary with the size and complexity of the population encompassed. The larger a unit is, and the more intensively specialized and wealthy its industries and its people are, the greater the number and kinds of groups within its borders. This is why the densely populated industrial states and the large cities often contain the entire array. But anyone who thinks smaller communities and sparsely settled states are free from non-governmental pressures has probably failed to examine them carefully and objectively. Often, legitimate non-governmental groups are denounced along with the illicit groups; in point of fact, no government without legitimate groups can meaningfully be called democratic, which is why the authors of the Bill of Rights took pains to include the right "to petition the Government for a redress of grievances" among the guarantees of the First Amendment.

Given all the differences among non-governmental groups and their distribution over the political landscape, in what sense can they be treated as members of a single category? Simply this: They do not have the power to issue official decisions in the way parties do, officials do, and even bureaucrats do. They often wield strong influence over persons who *are* empowered to promulgate authoritative decisions, but neither in law nor in practice can they produce documents that will elicit the widespread kind of obedience evoked by these other participants. What non-governmental groups try to do, and the manner in which they try to do it, both originate to a considerable extent in the special position they occupy, which is characteristic of all of them.

In the American system the decisions of every unit of government also reflect the influences exerted by other units of government. Formal channels of influence abound, as they must in a system where functions are divided and where inescapable ambiguities and overlapping attend the division. In addition, there are many informal channels. Some emerge because of the mere physical proximity of officers and employees of all levels—local, state, and national. Practically every square mile, and every citizen, is under not just two or three units of government, but usually under several, often under dozens, and occasionally under scores, so contact is inevitable. Other channels develop through the specialized professional and technical societies to which the officials and bureaucrats in the same kind of work at different levels belong, through their common training and their conferences, and through their contact with one another in the ordinary performance of their daily tasks. Moreover, parties span the tiers of government. All together, these factors create an interplay among decisions and actions taken at each level, and, at any level, by neighboring, competing, and co-operating units.

Chances are the electorate, as a collectivity, constitutes the most influential group of people in politics. Through its ability to turn incumbents out of office, it can disrupt all sorts of political bargains and settlements among all the participants, compelling them to revise their strategies and even their goals, and elevating some to dominant positions while consigning others to oblivion, at least temporarily. Commentators sometimes deride the electorate, regarding it as easily manipulated and sheeplike in its behavior. But elections do spring surprises, and even candidates in safe constituencies often experience considerable uncertainty as they face their tests at the polls. It is this uncertainty that forces all the participants in politics to keep one eye warily on the electorate, and all who enjoy extensive electoral support (or can convince others they do) command respect throughout the political system. So everyone at one time or another courts the electorate and invites its backing.

Yet the electorate cannot be treated as a participant in the same sense as the others. For it is a heterogeneous body, and the relation between its actions and the day-to-day actions of the officials it chooses is so remote and complicated that there is no way of ascertaining what precisely its mandates are, what claims it makes, what prizes it seeks, and whether its demands are satisfied. Perhaps the electorate does nothing more than indicate its discontent vaguely by unseating those in office. Without being a seeker of the stakes of politics, it thus colors everything all the seekers do.

The electorate does resemble the other categories in one important respect: it is not monolithic. Many of the different offices each voter casts his ballot for embrace different constituencies, follow different boundary lines. Consequently, the individual voter is a member of several different aggregates of voters at the same time. Moreover, the number of voters who turn out for an election is always related to the prominence of the highest office at stake (usually the chief executive position); consequently, the vote for a congressman in a presidential year, for example, is apt to be much larger than the mid-term vote. The same situation applies to other offices, state and local; the electoral cycle in this country is almost everywhere a four-year one, with presidential elections calling forth the largest vote, state and local elections the next largest, and off-year elections when no chief executive post is at stake the smallest. One would be justified, therefore, in speaking of "electorates" rather than "the electorate"; "the electorate," too, is a multifarious collection of sub-sets.

Striving for the stakes and prizes of political action would certainly deteriorate into chaotic and mutually destructive warfare were it not conducted within a framework of written and customary rules, and even more important, within a broad area of consensus. There is agreement as well as conflict, cooperation as well as competition. In the last analysis, the commitment to the maintenance of the system ordinarily outruns any short-term gain available to any particular participant or group of participants. Everyone's in politics, but, hopefully, not necessarily to the bitter end.

80

Everyone's in Politics

Everyone is not in politics to the same extent, however. Some contestants for the stakes take part in decisions over virtually the entire spectrum of governmental activity. No function, no service, no program, no procedure, no question of organization is inconsequential to them, sometimes because their self-defined sphere of interest is so inclusive, sometimes because the system forces them to face all kinds of questions whether they like them or not.

Other contestants enter the fray only when narrow matters are involved. They concern themselves with only a limited band of the total spectrum, and occasionally even with only one particular issue.

In like fashion, some contestants are on the scene all the time. They are constant surveyors of political developments in which they are interested. Others are more intermittent and even erratic in their appearances, and many turn up only once, in connection with specific matters so vital to them as to overcome their normal apathy and goad them to action.

FIGURE 1. *Patterns of participation in governmental decision-making.* (Adapted from Wallace S. Sayre and Herbert Kaufman, *Governing New York City* (New York: Russell Sage Foundation, 1960), p. 79.)

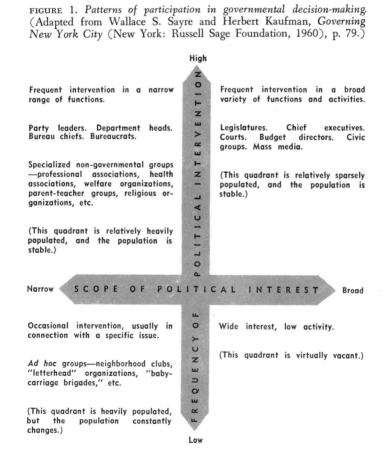

High

POLITICAL INTERVENTION

Frequent intervention in a narrow range of functions.

Party leaders. Department heads. Bureau chiefs. Bureaucrats.

Specialized non-governmental groups —professional associations, health associations, welfare organizations, parent-teacher groups, religious organizations, etc.

(This quadrant is relatively heavily populated, and the population is stable.)

Frequent intervention in a broad variety of functions and activities.

Legislatures. Chief executives. Courts. Budget directors. Civic groups. Mass media.

(This quadrant is relatively sparsely populated, and the population is stable.)

Narrow ← SCOPE OF POLITICAL INTEREST → **Broad**

FREQUENCY OF

Occasional intervention, usually in connection with a specific issue.

Ad hoc groups—neighborhood clubs, "letterhead" organizations, "baby-carriage brigades," etc.

(This quadrant is heavily populated, but the population constantly changes.)

Wide interest, low activity.

(This quadrant is virtually vacant.)

Low

81

Everyone's in Politics

Thus, our analysis of political participants requires further refinement if we are to explore all the dimensions of state and local government and politics. We must deepen our understanding by comparing the participants according to the scope and frequency of their intervention in the political process (see Fig. 1).

BROAD SCOPE, HIGH FREQUENCY

Surprisingly few participants in any of the categories intervene in a wide range of subjects consistently. Among officials, it is chiefly the general organs of government—the legislative bodies, the chief executives (and their personal staffs), and the higher courts that are continuously involved. The scope of their activities covers virtually everything their respective governments do.

In legislative bodies, for example, this breadth arises from the fact that most governmental activities rest on a base of state statutes and local laws. In a state legislature a single session may bring across the legislators' desks bills on banking, highways, taxes, utilities, welfare, education, traffic, health, agriculture, natural resources, and hundreds of other subjects, as new programs are proposed, old ones modified or repealed. Hardly any phase of modern life escapes their attention; everything lies within their purview. The states have not delegated to local governments the authority to act in all these fields, so local legislative discretion is quite a bit narrower. For city councils, county boards, and town or township meetings alike, however, legislative discretion is as broad as the whole expanse of local government, however restricted that expanse may be.

The province of state and local chief executives is correspondingly extensive. Indeed, even when chief executives are not really empowered to act in a field—as mayors, for example, are often hampered by machinery and tradition that requires them to keep their hands off education—they are likely to be blamed for any troubles or weaknesses in that field by other participants and by the electorate. So governors, mayors, city managers, presidents of county boards, first selectmen, and other executives are drawn into all subjects no matter what their individual inclinations and preferences might be. Indeed, if they review the bills passed by their respective legislative bodies, their area of concern is at least equal to that of their coordinate branch. Some executives see these responsibilities only as burdens; more experienced ones see them also as opportunities that keep the executives constantly in the public eye, afford them leverage for bargaining with all other participants, and permit them to promote those programs in which they have a special personal interest. If executives have huge perimeters to defend, they also have huge preserves in which to maneuver.

In a society that prides itself on having a government of laws, it is not altogether unexpected that practically everything ends up in the courts. At the lower levels, courts are quite specialized. There are civil courts, criminal courts, probate courts, sometimes separate courts of domestic relations, and others, sometimes with added specialization within these units. Moreover, significant and serious cases are reserved for higher courts to decide. Some courts try cases; some try cases and also hear appeals from lower courts; some only hear appeals. In every state, however, there

82

Everyone's in Politics

is a high court (usually, but not always, called a supreme court) from which there is no further judicial appeal.[8] Handling only appeals (except for some technical exception with which we need not be concerned here), the high courts may be asked to rule on a wide variety of subjects, and, although they themselves decide what they will review and what they will not, every term may bring cases before them which range from the constitutionality of major legislation under the state constitution to reviewing the conviction of an alleged traffic violator. So, like their counterparts in other governmental branches, the highest judges find themselves reaching decisions on all phases of human life and on all aspects of governmental operations. They cannot, in the same manner as the other branches, take the initiative themselves; cases must be brought before them before they can rule. But, it is an unusual facet of government that is not sooner or later tested in court.

Perhaps one other kind of official ought to be added to this list: budget officers, where they are found. (Today, specialized budget officers are found in most larger jurisdictions, but they are rather unusual in smaller ones). Theoretically, a budget office is concerned only with estimating expenditures and then with managing the expenditures after the budget has been enacted into law. Actually, a budget is the fiscal embodiment of substantive decisions on policy, organization, and procedure. When we know how much money is allocated to each program, to which agencies the money goes for carrying out the program, and what terms and conditions are attached, we have touched on virtually every corner of government. As a matter of fact, budget officers usually have power to approve the creation of new positions, so personnel as well as policy questions fall within their authority. Although budget officers are often criticized by heads of other agencies for their allegedly narrow accounting approach to problems of substantive policy in which they are not expert, the very frequency of the comment from so many diverse departments is itself testimony to the scope of budgetary intervention and influence.

Practically the only other contestants for political stakes who are interested in a broad range of issues and are frequent participants in politics are civic groups and the mass media—particularly the newspapers. On the whole, governmentally oriented civic and reform groups are found in state capitals, cities, and suburbs far more frequently than in non-urban areas, but they are not unknown in these sections. Wherever they exist, they tend to assume the role of self-appointed guardians of the formal machinery, procedures, and rules of the governmental process. This statement does not mean they never appear as advocates of change; quite the contrary. But their chief means of achieving their objectives is to alter established governmental structures or to compel other participants to observe to the letter the requirements of the rules. So they turn up everywhere, now urging structural and procedural revisions, now taking one de-

[8] Appeals may be taken from the highest courts of the states to the Supreme Court of the United States, but the Supreme Court does not review all such appeals by any means, and under no circumstances will it accept jurisdiction of a case that does not in the opinion of the justices involve a "federal question." For a brief summary of federal judicial jurisdiction, see Robert K. Carr, Marver H. Bernstein, Donald H. Morrison, and Joseph E. McLean, *American Democracy in Theory and Practice*, 3rd ed. (New York: Rinehart, 1959), pp. 462–463.

Everyone's in Politics

partment or another to task, now evaluating candidates for office or the records of incumbents, now whipping up public indignation by charges of ineptitude or scandal in the conduct of government generally or of particular programs specifically. In larger jurisdictions they are constantly on the scene, and although they are able, as public officers are not, to be highly selective about decisions they will concentrate their attention on, they end up by becoming involved (albeit with somewhat lower frequency) in almost as great a variety of problems.

We can speak similarly about newspapers. An editor, a columnist, or a reporter may pick up almost any decision or program or event and make a public issue of it. For the most part, newspapers tend to stress the spectacular; honesty, efficiency, and agreement do not, according to the canons of journalism, "make news." An exposé, a critical series, a battle—these help in the causes of increased circulation, civic improvement, and self-advancement simultaneously. So the representatives of the fourth estate hunt for these things, and it would not be an exaggeration to say they try to provoke controversy at times, partly to generate stories and partly to break open stories they suspect but lack information about. No aspect of government and politics is immune; newspapers may seize or fix on almost anything.

Over and above their special feature items, the newspapers in their routine coverage create public images of men in politics. In their pages a public figure may be projected as a man of vigor, integrity, and statesmanship, or as negligent, suspect, and self-seeking. An agency may be portrayed as businesslike and dedicated, or bungling and ridden with corruption. A man may be lifted from obscurity to prominence. Day by day, sometimes without knowing it, the working members of the mass communications industries paint the picture of the men, organizations, and issues in politics that guide the activities of all other participants and of the public at large. And in the case of state and local politics, it is the press more than any other single medium that performs this function.

Neither the press nor any other mass medium nor any combination of them controls governments, parties, or elections. Not only are they merely one among many participants in the search for political stakes, but other participants have learned to make use of the mass media for purposes of their own; communications people are not the masters of the governmental process in America. They *are,* however, very significant elements in that process, and their role in it is broad and continuous.

NARROW SCOPE, HIGH FREQUENCY

A much larger proportion of the participants are highly and continuously active but confine their attention and energies to a limited band of the whole governmental and political spectrum.

Party leaders are among those individuals or groups who fall under this heading. Traditionally, their main concern has been with the nomination, election, and appointment of public personnel, with the procedures by which such selections are made, and with such decisions as affect their organizational and individual welfare. In other substantive policy problems they have *not* generally been interested. To be sure, on behalf of a

Everyone's in Politics

supporter, they may approach officials to urge a particular line of action, or to block or modify a policy, or, most frequently, to secure an individual exception from the application of a policy. In their role as intermediaries party leaders may be called on to intervene in a wide sweep of functional fields, and their concentration on patronage may similarly involve them in many kinds of governmental programs. Ultimately, though, their distinctive attribute is their unique position in the electoral process, from which all their other influence derives. In this fundamental sense, their focus is narrow.

Their activity, however, is incessant. The bargaining, negotiating, fighting, compromising, conciliating, arbitrating, and maneuvering over choosing nominees, campaigning for candidates, obtaining appointments, and winning favors for constituents never stop. These activities rise to a fever pitch as election time approaches, but even when they subside to their normal level they remain quite intense. The parties' front is narrow, but never quiet.

This trait is shared by numerous other contestants for the stakes of politics, but in connection with other bands of the spectrum. The administrator of each functionally specialized line agency (i.e., those that serve the public directly, such as education, police, fire, health, welfare, sanitation, and the like) and each staff or overhead agency (i.e., budget, personnel management, law, purchasing, and so on) applies himself almost exclusively to the program for which he has prime responsibility, and is apt to take note of what goes on in other fields only when what happens there impinges on his tasks. The bureaucracy of each agency also reflects this specialized span of interest, and so do the professional and technical associations (the bar, the doctors, highway engineers, sanitarians, and so forth) whose occupational concerns are linked largely to only a single program. The clientele served and/or regulated by an agency will often be organized (in parent-teachers associations, for example, or in industrial and trade associations, or in associations of homeowners or neighborhood residents), and private or religious organizations performing parallel services (e.g., schools; hospitals; charitable groups; settlement houses; health associations, such as heart funds, cancer societies, tuberculosis associations, and so on) will generally display marked interest in what happens to or is done by their public counterparts. Financial questions are closely watched by taxpayers groups, bondholders associations, and banks.

These clusters of functional organizations and individuals bridge the lines of governmental jurisdiction. In welfare, for instance, or highways, federal officers and employees are in contact with their corresponding specialists at the state level, while the state men maintain liaison with their local counterparts. At the same time, specialists at lower levels often bring pressure to bear on higher-ups, and it is not unknown for local officers to attempt to bypass relevant state agencies in reaching for federal assistance. Also, the actions of neighboring jurisdictions, or competing governments (competing, for example, by making tax concessions to industry in order to attract it), do not escape notice, and may lead to reprisals or other forms of pressure. In other words, in the functional arenas of each unit of government, the officials and bureaucrats of other governments must be reckoned as active and influential participants, especially as "vertical combinations" of specialists—i.e., organizations uniting specialists at all

85

levels of government—gain steadily in strength and status.

Everything that goes on in one of these functional fields matters to all these participants. Events outside their circumscribed area of interest seldom induce them to respond forcefully, even when the events are of major dimensions. Within their areas, decisions and actions trivial to outsiders may stimulate impassioned reactions. These areas are thus well-populated, and by groups whose activity never lets up.

NARROW SCOPE, LOW FREQUENCY

No student of politics can fail to be impressed by the number of *ad hoc* groups that spring into existence in connection with a specific action or decision (more often to oppose than to propose) and then vanish from the political arena. Sometimes the members come together solely to influence an official decision, and then dissolve completely. Sometimes they are permanent organizations for which politics is not a major consideration, but which are sufficiently provoked by some issue to take political action on but one occasion. In either case, though they lack political staying power, they may for a brief time bring great weight to bear, and the political calculations of all the more enduring participants may be upset unless they accurately gauge the probabilities that such groups will form and correctly estimate the power they may be able to wield.

All sorts of issues give rise to such groups—the location of a school; the desire for additional school-bus service; the route of a highway or a through street; the kinds of books in the public library; the proposal to add fluorides to water; a variation from a zoning regulation; a special assessment; construction of a park or playground; a request by a railroad for permission to curtail service; a change in route or schedules by franchised bus operators. Taken one by one, none of these decisions is particularly noteworthy; taken together, they add up to a good deal of policy-making.

Ad hoc groups do not necessarily confine themselves to limited questions. When they deal with broader matters in more general terms, however, they enter arenas with more experienced, better financed, better known, and more knowledgeable organizations. Under those conditions their effectiveness is sharply reduced. When they mobilize to influence a single act, whether they consist of nothing more than a handful of people with letterheads and a typewriter or a substantial membership brought to a meeting or hearing in a body by enterprising leaders, they can exert a profound effect on the outcome.

DIFFERENTIAL PATTERNS

One point suggested briefly in an earlier section of this discussion warrants repeating: not all the groups and varieties of participation described in this book will be found in every state and in every community. In any large industrial state, in any of the larger cities, in many of the urban counties, and in the suburbs, all the complexities outlined here will undoubtedly exist. Indeed, this picture may represent a simplification compared to reality. In less populous states and in smaller communities, where industry and commerce are less diversified, where the population is fairly

Everyone's in Politics

homogeneous, where office seeks men rather than men seeking office, where government performs only the old and traditional services, where there is no inter-party competition, where the social forces making for conformity deter expression of existing differences, where labor is unorganized and unselfconscious, where minorities are systematically denied their political and civic rights, there may well be far less interaction among differentiated groups than is here suggested. In some small communities a comparatively tight inner circle consisting of the local industrialist, the largest farmers and real estate owners, the chief merchants, the banker and the lawyer, and the oldest families may dominate the governmental process without serious political challenge from any quarter.

The difference here may be merely one of degree. The divisions and rivalries within these communities may be fewer and the contestants less clearly defined, but the same forces might be at work in a rudimentary way. On the other hand, a difference in degree, if large enough, may become a difference in kind. The descriptive model set forth in these pages would in this case be inapplicable to such communities, or would at least require very extensive qualification to make it applicable. Until probative evidence is available, the question must remain open.

In those more developed states and localities where the kind of diversity here depicted does obtain, one impressive feature of the system is the abundance of specialized and particular aims and the sparsity of participants whose concerns embrace the entire realm of governmental operation instead of just parts. The problems created by this state of affairs will be taken up later, but special notice should be taken of this quality of the political process.

The "Great Game"

State and local governments yield up to those who seek them all sorts of rewards. Moreover, those who neglect opportunities to influence state and local governmental decisions and actions may suffer severe deprivations, not only in the political realm but in the economic sphere as well. Consequently, the reward-seekers, the individuals and groups who try to register their views on the decisions that flow from state and local political systems, include almost everybody. Of course, everybody does not take part to the same extent in the process by which decisions are shaped; there are many varieties of participation. But, loosely speaking, everyone participates to some degree at some time. The "great game of politics" has become one of the standard clichés of our time for referring to the governmental process, and like many clichés it embodies a profoundly useful idea. But the game is not a spectator sport; even the observers get drawn into the game.

To take part in a game or contest is to pursue a strategy—sometimes inadvertently, sometimes without planning, sometimes without making a move (all of which may confuse other competitors; hence beginner's luck), but more often calculatedly and deliberately. When the stakes are high and the opportunities for maneuver seem endless, the strategies may become intricate and ingenious. In state and local politics that is exactly what has happened. We turn in the next chapter to the political strategies there developed.

87

Political
Strategies

If we regard political strategies as courses
of action devised and pursued by participants in the contest
for political stakes to increase the share they obtain for themselves
or those they favor, the widely varied array of strategies may
conveniently be grouped into three classes:
(1) those designed to determine who gets public office and employment;
(2) those designed to manipulate the structure and procedure
of governments and parties; and (3) those
designed to influence policy deliberations, policy
adoptions, and policy enforcement *regardless* of who is in office and of
organization and procedure.

If you could pick all the men in official and bureaucratic positions in a government without having to consult anyone else and without having to satisfy any other demands besides your own, if you knew intimately the personal and professional qualities of all the men you picked, and if you could replace at will any men whose behavior did not conform to your expectations and desires, you would probably find it unnecessary to exert any other kinds of influence on their day-by-day behavior in order to get the kinds of decisions and action you wanted from them. By the very process of choosing them, you would be determining what would happen.

Even under the most dictatorial systems, no such total control of personnel occurs. Even the dictator discovers he has powerful groups and factions to appease, and, in any event, he cannot know everyone and every job, so he is compelled to rely on the judgment of others. In a democratic system procedures are established with a view to making the choice of personnel *deliberately* open and subject to negotiation and bargaining so that *many* elements of the population can inject their own spokesmen into inner political circles. The underlying premise is the same in both cases: who selects the rulers also shapes the character of public policies and programs. The differences between the two systems are in large part the result of differences in the number who take part in these selections.

In a democratic society everyone concerned with the stakes of politics is likely at one time or another to make an effort to see that those positions in government and party are filled by men who will do what their supporters wish. Of course, as we mentioned in another section, very few participants manifest much interest in the full range of public functions; most are concerned only with the narrow portions of this range that affect them personally. Similarly, most groups concentrate more intensely on only the *relevant* positions rather than on *all* the important posts. (In any case, even if restricted interest did not limit the extent of ambition, the dictates of economy of effort would; most political strategists are too shrewd to squander their resources by spreading them too thin.) As a result, not only nominations and elections, but appointments and removals as well, generally involve aggressively maneuvering forces.

NOMINATIONS

The dominant method of nominating candidates for elective office at all levels of government throughout the country is the direct primary. Only in a few states are some nominees still selected by conventions.[1]

Primaries apparently got their start in one-party areas (and many states and localities outside the South are also of this character) where, with no opposition to the majority party, nomination was tantamount to election to office, so popular participation had to be introduced into nominating procedures if there were to be any popular election at all. The primary was

[1] And even in these cases, the delegates to the conventions are ordinarily elected in primaries.

first developed in the Democratic South, but it first became state law in Republican Wisconsin and other midwestern and western states.[2]

Primaries then spread because of pressure by reformers who felt conventions dominated by the inner circles of party organizations did not select candidates who really reflected the sentiments of the people, and thus deprived the voters of genuine choices at the polls. By holding party elections in which all the members of each party (the "closed" primary)[3] or in some cases any qualified voter (the "open" primary and the "blanket" primary) are entitled to vote for the selection of party nominees and party leaders, the reformers hoped to break the power of the party bosses.

Expert opinion seems to have moved to the conclusion that primaries *have* in fact weakened the influence of party leaders in most jurisdictions. Indeed, in some one-party areas, party leadership is almost nonexistent; it is easy to get on the primary ballots, so voters in the primary end up choosing blindly among many candidates, having little idea of what they stand for or what their relations to the rest of the ticket will be. The final slate of candidates, who are assured of election, may be assembled from a variety of factions, many of them relatively unknown if not downright hostile to one another.

In two-party areas, the story is a little different. Since very few of the party members eligible to vote in primaries actually turn out even for widely publicized contests within each party, the party leaders are usually able to secure nomination of their choices by making sure that their loyal followers cast ballots; a small number of such followers often decides the outcome when few people turn out to vote in the primary. So party leaders in these areas have managed to maintain *some* of the power their predecessors wielded under the convention system. At the same time, the primaries encourage insurgents and other factions to challenge the established leadership more frequently than was the case under conventions. Moreover, since aspirants to elective office are more likely to seek nomination by the party which seems most likely to win, primary fights are more common in the favored party and may draw attention and following from the minority party, thereby still further weakening the two-party system and the remnants of party discipline it preserves.[4]

These conditions do not mean that party leaders are utterly impotent, but they do mean that other participants in politics are now able in most places to exert influence on the choice of candidates by the parties. In one-party areas the leaders of factions court the moral and material support of private citizens and non-governmental groups whose assistance they covet, and presumably may not hesitate to bargain vigorously for such aid. Newspaper support can be crucial for a campaign, so factional leaders are also vulnerable to pressure from these quarters. In two-party areas the necessity

[2] V. O. Key, Jr., *Politics, Parties, and Pressure Groups*, 4th ed. (New York: Crowell, 1958), pp. 411–412.

[3] In a closed primary voters must be registered members of the party for whose nominees and officers they wish to vote. In an open primary, which is much less common, voters may select at will the party for whose nominees and officers they wish to vote; no registration or other indication of membership is required. The blanket primary is used only in Washington; the voters may shift from party to party from one office to the next, although they may not vote for more than one candidate for any public or party office.

[4] Key, *op. cit.*, pp. 413–433.

Political Strategies

to submit to party discipline in order to win general elections gives party leaders a degree of freedom in the nominating process that their one-party counterparts do not enjoy, but the need to conciliate as many groups as possible in order not to lose elections compels them, too, to respond to demands of all sorts of groups in their constituencies and to invite coverage and favorable comment in the mass media. Moreover, the truly competitive election is apt to cost more than even a hotly contested primary, so the parties cannot afford to cut themselves off from potential sources of revenue. Everywhere, then, in varying degree, nominations, though formally made by the parties, reflect the claims of other participants in the contest for the stakes of politics.

This statement is especially true when nominations seek candidates rather than vice versa. Parties with slim chances of victory, and contesting only for minor offices, do not generally succeed in attracting eager hopefuls. Candidates may have to be induced to accept nomination, and, in such situations, parties are often inclined to ratify anyone willing to run no matter who puts his name forward. Outside groups will often prove particularly influential in nominating candidates when this is the case.

In third and other minor parties, the party leaders are usually in virtually full control of the nominating process. Whether united by ideological commitments or by rebellion against established parties, the leaders, because they ordinarily cannot hope to win, tend to be more concerned with assembling just enough of a following to swing elections than with aggregating enough votes for a majority. Since they keep the party reins in the hands of like-minded colleagues, and do not aim for mass support, they do not feel obliged to accommodate many outside demands. In fact, election victories might divide them into factions. So they play a minority role, trying to build up as much leverage as they can to bargain with the major party or parties without diluting their own programs, and without jeopardizing their own control of their organizations.

Generally speaking, party leaders collectively are probably the most influential group in selecting nominees. But nowhere do they have a complete monopoly (save in some third and minor parties), and everywhere they take into account the claims of ethnic and religious and national-origin organizations, regional and neighborhood and other geographical demands, newspaper and other mass media suggestions, the clamor of reform groups, and the views of major supporters and many other participants. All who can do so bring to bear all the leverage they can muster to influence the nominating process.

ELECTIONS

Deciding who will occupy the elective seats of government is a function only the electorate can perform. Even where there is only one effective party, it is not until a general election has been held that the victorious candidates are inaugurated. The electorate alone is authorized to determine which legally qualified nominees will legitimately ascend to elective office.

All other participants therefore bend their efforts toward trying to influence the behavior of the voters. In one-party areas campaigns may

Political Strategies

be little more than token gestures on the part of all candidates. In two-party areas the burden of campaigning for minor offices may fall more heavily on the candidates themselves and on their personal friends than on any organization, although party label may carry more weight here than any other single factor. For the more important, more visible offices in two-party areas, campaigning becomes energetic, elaborate, and expensive, with neither side letting up for fear the other might gain an advantage. Here is where the most diverse assortment of groups appears.

Techniques of influencing the electorate reduce themselves to two basic strategies: (1) personal contact with the voters and (2) publicity. Personal contact is a specialty of party organizations; it is the job of their field workers to get in touch with as many voters as they can—to recruit new supporters if possible, to bring out the regulars in any case, and to collect signatures on designating or nomination petitions when necessary. Particularly when statewide offices (including presidential electors) are at stake, the party organizations are likely to welcome voluntary help on an individual basis and on a group basis (supplied, for example, by labor unions). On the other hand, these are precisely the times when supplementary organizations—"Citizens for X," "Independents for Y," "Volunteers for Z"—are likely to appear, so the influence of the party even in establishing personal contact may be diluted by these parallel structures.[5] Generally, however, these supplementary groups lack the staying power and the settled lines of communication of the parties, and their impact is at best intermittent even though they may be particularly influential in a single campaign. Consequently, the party organizations tend in the long run to remain the prime instruments for personal liaison with voters for most state and local party candidates.

Publicity—the art of getting the names, qualifications, and policies of candidates before the electorate in the most flattering light—is another matter. Here, the parties have no monopoly. For state and local offices the press is crucial, and both television and radio also play important parts. In addition, large organizations have their own internal house organs and other newspapers for reaching their own memberships and perhaps wider audiences as well. Civic and reform groups publish evaluations of candidates and of programs, and send this information to persons they consider "opinion leaders." Religious and ethnic associations may do the same. Parties themselves organize rallies, send out speakers, finance broadcasts, post placards and billboard advertisements, mail campaign circulars, and engage in a host of other public-relations undertakings to carry the word to the electorate. In fact, parties probably engage in this kind of activity far more than any other single category of participants. But in the public-relations aspects of election campaigns, parties share parts of the stage with a great many others.

The strategies of the participants thus include efforts to influence the behavior of the electorate in competitive elections. It is by no means clear that these endeavors really determine the outcome of elections, specially

---

[5] As a matter of fact, however, the parallel structures are often established by the regular parties themselves in order to attract voters who cannot bring themselves to support a party although they may want to vote for its candidate. For the same reason, the parties often set up "independent" parties to support their candidates, who thus benefit from additional lines on the ballot.

Political Strategies

since factors beyond party control (the business cycle, national as well as state and local emergencies and crises, international tensions, population shifts and changes) often seem to move voters in not altogether predictable directions. Still, the circumstantial evidence suggests that attempts to influence electorates have some effect, and that neglect of this strategy by any group might thereby give an advantage to other groups. So election strategy will doubtless remain prominent in the political behavior of all participants who have the resources to pursue it.

APPOINTMENTS AND REMOVALS[6]

Of the slightly less than 6 million state and local officeholders in this country, probably well over 90 per cent are appointed to office, some by elected officials, the others by higher ranking appointed officials. Thus all who try to influence the selection of governmental personnel at some time turn their attention to the process of appointment.

Rarely, therefore, does an appointing officer have an opportunity to make a selection that is his own free choice. From his point of view a vacancy may appear as an asset, a chance to strengthen his own hand, promote his own program, advance his own career, or all three. To other officials, however, it may be an occasion to press for the selection of personnel with whom they will find it easy to work in carrying out their own responsibilities. To party leaders vacancies are rewards they can bestow on loyal followers and supporters. To non-governmental groups of all kinds, vacancies present an opportunity to assure the presence of sympathetic officeholders in strategic places, or at least a channel of access to such strategically placed individuals. To bureaucrats, they mean a chance to parade their arguments for "career service" and "non-political selection," meaning that such vacancies should be filled from the top of their own ranks. The press and civic groups will see here a possibility of insisting that their brand of virtue and competence be reflected in public appointments, and of airing their views in such a way that the appointing officer ignores them at his peril. At the same time, there may be several candidates vying for the job, which is to them a prize to be sought, a means of rendering public service, and a road to greater influence and advancement in the future. Consequently, when a vacancy occurs, the official with the authority to fill it is likely to find himself the object of attention on the part of many participants in the political process. Naturally, all positions are not equally prized, and some considered important to some groups in some areas (such as a school principal or an assistant district attorney) may be relatively trivial to others. Only the very highest are likely to attract a wide variety of participants. Still, many appointments, including some of rather low rank, generate surprising competition.

The common strategy is to confine the discretion of appointing officers to limited categories of eligibles, or (more rarely) even to specific individuals. Civil-service requirements are the best-known method of accomplishing this end, and have reduced the relative influence of party

[6] For a fuller discussion of these processes see Wallace S. Sayre and Herbert Kaufman, *Governing New York City* (New York: Russell Sage Foundation, 1960), Chapter VII.

Political Strategies

organizations while enhancing the power of personnel specialists, bureaucracies, and some non-governmental groups. Another method is to prescribe qualifications for appointees, such as medical degrees for public-health officers, admission to the bar for legal and investigatory posts, engineering degrees for public-works appointments, and so on. Similarly, residence and bipartisan requirements cover appointments to some boards and commissions. In general, these provisions also strike at the parties, while improving the relative position of non-governmental groups, especially of particular professions and occupations. Often, what groups are not able to achieve by formal legal provisions, they sometimes achieve in fact, so that financial officers are often accountants or bankers or businessmen, welfare officials are social workers, and ethnic and religious groups are often recognized as having special claim on particular jobs. Occasionally an organization has veto powers over candidates for appointments to some positions, or at least the traditional right to be consulted before the appointment is announced. By adept timing and formation of coalitions, some groups succeed in putting forth a list of names from which the appointer is expected or required to choose (as in the Missouri plan of naming judges, which we discussed earlier), and at times may even be able to offer a single name that the appointing officer rejects only at considerable risk of controversy and criticism.

Appointments, then, no less than nominations and elections, represent compromises and settlements among many interested participants. Since everyone recognizes the value of having in office men who are "right" for the job from their point of view, no part of the selection process escapes their notice.

Similarly, the removal powers of appointing officers are hedged about with restraints. Many of these restraints are formal; removal must be for cause, and often only after notice and a hearing, with ultimate appeal to the courts. Even where some of an appointing officer's subordinates serve "at his pleasure," however, he may find removal a sizeable political hazard because of the groups it stirs up, and because appointing a successor may involve still larger battles. In point of fact, appointing officers have and use less drastic disciplinary measures than removal, and are more apt to use them than the ultimate weapon. Moreover, they can often exact a "voluntary" resignation when an exercise of the removal power itself would be difficult. So the authority is seldom employed. But possessing it, appointing officers are able to negotiate solutions in situations which would otherwise afford them little bargaining power.

The recall is a special removal procedure, usually applied to elective rather than appointive officers, but sometimes applied to the latter as well. Under it, a small percentage of the voters may petition to remove a public officer before the expiration of his regular term and force an election to fill the vacancy. The issue must then be placed before the electorate for decision. Provisions for the recall are common at the local level, and some dozen states have also adopted the device.[7] Used comparatively sparingly, even at the local level, it is a controversial procedure stemming from an earlier era in our history. In any event, when it is brought into play,

[7] Jewell Cass Phillips, *State and Local Government in America* (New York: American Book Co., 1954), p. 128.

Political Strategies

it certainly engenders the same sort of interaction among the participants in the governmental process that we have seen prevailing in other phases of the selection of public personnel. Whenever the participants have the chance to help determine who will receive a public appointment, they seize that chance.

Manipulating Structure and Procedure

Participants in politics also endeavor to manipulate the structure and procedures of governmental and party organizations in order to facilitate their access to, and augment their influence on, officials and party decision-making regardless of who sits in the key places. In Chapter 2 we saw that political organization in this country can be interpreted in terms of a sequence of values. Although a broad consensus certainly did seem to govern during each historical period, the specific mechanisms through which it was expressed were arrived at by the interplay of many participants in the governmental process, all striving to impress their own perspectives and goals on the actions and decisions flowing from parties, bureaucracies, and officialdom.

For obvious reasons, proposals for modifying structure and procedure are usually cast in language that stresses the high moral purposes of the proponents and the rich benefits these proposals will bestow on all members of the community. Advocates of new plans speak of efficiency, excluding incompetents, preventing dishonesty, improving administration. Seldom do they make explicit how the recommended changes will affect the relative influence of the various contestants who are seeking the stakes of political action. This is not to say that the motives of the advocates are *not* lofty, or the consequences *not* widely beneficial. But certainly every alteration in the way governments and parties are organized and operate transforms in some way the standing of the contestants and their capacity to shape the content and effect of decisions and actions. And, although some who argue for or against particular changes have in mind only broad ethical and community-wide goals, many others are aware of the impact the plans will have on their respective positions in the contest.

And every change does have such an impact. The influence of party leaders has been progressively weakened by the move toward civil-service reforms, technical and professional requirements for officeholders, the introduction of specialized managerial experts as chief executives, the direct primary, and many other innovations of recent vintage. Correspondingly, bureaucracies, professional associations, and other groups have been able to exert greater leverage on decisions in their areas of expertise and special interest. Reducing party influence tends also to diminish the effectiveness of mass-membership organizations, whose large followings endow them with exceptional bargaining assets in the electoral arena, but whose capacity to apply pressure on "expert" administrators is far weaker. Agencies that serve and regulate narrow segments of the economy—railroads, utilities, traction companies, banks, insurance companies, labor and the like—quickly tend to identify with the activities they supervise, and the arrangements devised to safeguard their autonomy make it more difficult for other interests—especially consumers of these goods and services—

95

to break into the closed circle. A general department of conservation puts sportsmen, timber-using industries and professions, recreationists, and wilderness defenders in the same camp, so that at least one of these groups will probably feel its concept of resource utilization is being neglected by officials too responsive to their competitors, and will therefore advocate setting up a separate fish and wildlife commission, forestry bureau, or park department more amenable to its demands. When a minority party builds up enough of a following in a few districts to win in them consistently and thus to place its own critics and observers in the governing bodies of cities or counties, the majority party will frequently urge a switch from election by districts to election at large in order to isolate the pockets of minority strength and to prevent the minority party from capturing seats. If a group believes a locality is likely to be more severe in regulating the group than is the state in which it is located, the group can be expected to contend that this function cannot and should not be delegated away by the state. If, on the other hand, the group concludes that the locality will be less stringent than the state, it may well turn into an ardent patron of home rule. Every group tends to favor economy in the conduct of those services in which it has no stake, but to urge greater expenditures and expanded service when its interests are involved. A state or a locality will assail as "socialistic" a plan for federally aided medical insurance but will cheerfully accept the profits from a public liquor store monopoly or a municipal power plant. Ethnic and religious minorities find an ally and a shield in anti-discrimination commissions, but discriminatory employers, unions, landlords, hotel proprietors, and educational institutions, among others, raise questions about alleged invasions of their freedom. Reformers and the mass media favor provisions for public hearings on appointments, removals, legislation, and administrative rules because these hearings permit them to utilize their particular brand of influence most effectively.

This list can be indefinitely expanded, but there is no need to labor the point. No change in organization, no modification of procedure can be instituted without affecting some political participant. Those participants who have established effective lines of access and therefore exercise considerable influence on decisions that impinge on them almost invariably rise to the defense of the *status quo*. Those who feel excluded or ineffectual strive for revisions that will magnify their influence. If they have electoral strength, they extol the virtues of the ballot. If they are professional or technical specialists, they decry the interference of politicians. Structure and process become implements of political strategy as well as ends in themselves.

Furthermore, it is the strategy of almost every participant to make the structure and process he approves as enduring as possible. This tendency explains why so many decisions left to congressional discretion at the federal level are at the lower levels imbedded in state constitutions and city charters. Education, housing, welfare, civil service, and many other subjects are ordinarily regulated in substantial measure by provisions in these organic laws; these provisions represent victories for the supporters of these policies and programs. Similarly, limits on property taxes and governmental borrowing are protections won by property owners and bondholders. To secure the adoption of such provisions in a form most difficult

Political Strategies

to change is a challenge to their advocates, but, when such advocates can muster the strength to do so, they make the effort because success makes it easier for them later on to block attempts to reverse the policies. Not only organization and procedure, then, but the very kinds of documents in which organization and procedure are prescribed, become targets of groups that compete for the rewards of political action.

Influencing Policy Deliberations, Policy Adoptions, and Enforcement

A contestant may fail to influence the selection of officials and employees under whose jurisdiction he falls. He may even be defeated in his bid to manipulate structures and procedures in order to improve his chances of influencing the distribution of political rewards and prizes. Yet he still is by no means lacking in ways of impressing his views on the decision-making process. Regardless of who holds public office or employment, and regardless of the organization and procedures in effect, our system of government furnishes him with all sorts of opportunities to influence it.

PERSUASION

For one thing, there are many channels through which those concerned with a given decision may air their views and arguments and thus persuade others of the rightness of their cause. Few would contend that there is *no* sense of fair play and justice in the contest for political stakes. Although each participant pursues his own ends, and some aberrants casually and repeatedly ignore the well-being of their fellow citizens, the system functions within a boundary of tolerance, consensus, and mutual identification that inhibits extremists a great deal of the time and produces sympathetic reactions when some group is ridden over roughshod. Thus merely to make all contestants aware of what will happen if a proposed measure takes effect is sometimes enough to induce everyone to agree to amendments that will mitigate its effect, especially if the effect is not confined to a small number of people. Not all systems of government provide forums for such complaints; even in this country, in some states, Negroes, Mexican-Americans, Indians, and other minority groups encounter difficulty in influencing the calculations and compromises that shape policy. By and large, however, American state and local government is open and reasonably responsive to rational group defenses.

The most characteristic channel for ventilating contentions is the public hearing and systematic consultation with everyone involved in a particular decision. Legislative hearings are the most familiar type, particularly since some states require committee hearings on every bill before the bills are reported to the floor. But the legislature is not the sole platform for airing arguments. Investigating bodies, especially state bodies looking into local affairs, provide another outlet. Chief executives often seek advice both in formulating their programs and in determining what action to take on bills before they sign or veto them. Administrative agencies as a matter of course invite advice and criticism before issuing rules and regulations. Interested groups and individuals appear before all such officials when the chance presents itself.

97

Political Strategies

Thus a town or a county or a city or the highway department of a state normally invites expressions of views when selecting routes for roads and highways. A board of health will check on the impact of proposed food handling or food processing or cosmetic regulations, or similar issuances, before promulgating them; the industries governed by such regulations will have many suggestions to make. A zoning board will hold a hearing on requests for variances from zoning rules, or on adopting new rules and classifications. Public-service commissions may call in customers when deciding on changes in railroad service. Everywhere, and almost all the time, participants in the political process who wish to do so find occasions to make their positions known.

This privilege is not restricted to private organizations. Administrators and executives may plead for certain legislative measures just as private citizens and non-governmental groups do. One administrator may appear before other agencies to argue his case, as many do before budget officers when defending their estimates of expenses for the coming year. Legislators as individuals may serve as witnesses at hearings. Representatives of public employees will often speak for their constituents. Because they are on "the inside," officials and bureaucrats have certain advantages that other participants do not enjoy. At the same time, they operate under certain handicaps (especially a glare of publicity more relentless and searching than that to which most private groups are subject), which explains why in this analysis we treat them simply as another category of participants. In many important respects, they behave quite like other people who are not "in government."[8]

Formal appearances before official bodies are not the only way to present views. Frequently, participants in the same functional fields of governmental activity are in such close contact with one another that in an informal, casual way they exchange ideas and opinions. Many organizations deliberately cultivate access to, and voluntarily offer their services to, officials who will make the decision. Officials, for their part, often establish

---

[8] Many public officials and employees (below the top policy-determining positions) are restricted in their partisan political activities. At the state and local level, these limitations are generally less stringent than at the federal level, where civil-service legislation, and the Hatch Acts of 1939 and 1940, impose severe restraints and penalties. In 1939, however, an amendment to the Social Security Act required all states receiving federal welfare funds to develop state merit systems for employees paid entirely or in part out of these funds. And the Hatch Act of 1940 applied the prohibitions against partisan political activity to *all* state and local employees paid partly or wholly out of federal funds. In addition, state civil-service laws and "little Hatch Acts" often contain some restrictions on other state and local employees. So public servants do not enjoy *quite* the same freedom of action as other participants in the political process. See Paul P. Van Riper, *History of the United States Civil Service* (Evanston, Ill.: Row, Peterson, 1958), pp. 339–344; and H. Eliot Kaplan, *The Law of Civil Service* (New York: Matthew Bender, 1958), Chapter XII. For restrictions on state and local employees specifically, see Kaplan, *op. cit.*, pp. 343–350; Richard Christopherson, *Regulating Political Activities of Public Employees* (Chicago: Civil Service Assembly, Personnel Report No. 543, 1954); "'Little Hatch Acts' Provide Election-Time Do's and Don'ts for Public Servants." *Good Government* (bi-monthly bulletin of the National Civil Service League), Vol. LXX, No. 5 (September–October, 1953), pp. 42–46; Charles G. Pillon, "Political Activity by Public Employees," *Civil Service Law Reporter* (published by the National Civil Service League), Vol. 2, No. 11 (November, 1952), pp. 144–154.

Everyone's in Politics

advisory or consultative councils representing all the interests with whom they deal. Excessive reliance on informal contacts may subject officials to charges of collusion, so they are apt to be circumspect, if not secretive in soliciting opinions in this way. Formal public hearings are intended to offset, and perhaps to supplant, informal association of this kind. At the open discussion, people without personal access to public figures can nevertheless get the ear of officialdom, and they can see who else is doing so, and what policies are being urged. But everywhere there are informal lines of communication.

Most contestants (including, incidentally, public officials and party leaders) do not rely solely on personal appearances, whether formal or informal, to inject their grievances and desires into policy-making discussions. They seek coverage in the mass media, using press conferences, letters, and paid advertising. They publish their own materials. They work to get sympathetic editorial attention.[9] That is, what they cannot accomplish directly they attempt to achieve indirectly, which is one of the great advantages enjoyed by the mass media, and especially by the press (because it need not offer equal time to opposing views). The mass media can always set their own ideas before everyone, and from the opinions of other participants they can select the ones they want to publicize. Still, other groups, also, manage to disseminate their pleas and arguments.

Obviously, neither the best, nor the loudest, nor the most repeated arguments always prevail; many other factors underlie every political decision and action. But many participants have scored signal victories mainly on the basis of the force and persistence of their persuasive efforts. The method is also available even to those who possess no other important source of influence. It is therefore one of the most widely used of all the strategies for influencing deliberation, adoption, and enforcement of policy.

SUPPORT

Another strategy is lending support to participants whose past decisions and influence have been responsive to one's own demands and suggestions. This technique presumably creates an obligation to maintain such responsiveness in order to enjoy continued support. The whole process of policy formation is colored by calculations of what aid and assistance each participant can count on in case of conflict and controversy.

Support, in general, consists of public statements approving of, and commending, another participant at a strategic time—say, when that participant is embattled and under fire, or when he is seeking some decision against powerful and determined opposition. It may also mean using the other modes of influence described here to add to the other participant's own efforts to secure his end. Support is thus sometimes lent by groups to promote specific decisions in which they have no particular

9 Public officials, as well as non-governmental groups, employ this strategy. The official ceremonial ground-breaking and ribbon-cutting rites, the careful enumeration of responsible officers on signs and plaques on public improvements, the cultivation of a favorable press (including such devices as the exclusive interview, the briefing session, and the planted "leak"), and the spectacular, attention-getting declaration or charge are all illustrations of this practice.

interest purely for the purpose of rewarding their allies for past sympathy and solidarity, and to encourage such cooperation in the future.

Administrators are especially disposed to invoke support because their functional specialization creates for them more or less natural constituencies. They have their clientele, their professional associations, their bureaucracies, their parallel private organizations. A school superintendent, for instance, may be able to mobilize parents, educational societies, teachers, and neighborhood groups petitioning for more schools when he fights for his budget. A highway commissioner can turn to automobile owners' and truckers' and bus operators' associations, contractors, and perhaps to unions of construction workers. A planning body can usually bring out neighborhood organizations, property-owners' groups, professional planners, and civic societies. Every agency has its constituencies, and all rely on them for support at one time or another. To assure that support, they keep the interests of their constituents in mind as they go about their administrative tasks.

Administrators are not the only participants responsive to this type of inducement. Parties, after all, need voters and donors and workers to keep going. Elective officials need parties. Coalitions of non-governmental groups can of course accomplish what individual organizations ordinarily cannot, so they accede to one another. Bureaucrats often seek party backing for their demands, and may call on organized labor for assistance. Originators of new programs and policies often turn to official and bureaucratic experts to buttress their claims. Officials at one level of government solicit aid from officials at other levels, and it is not unusual for candidates in elections to importune respected public figures to intervene in the campaign on their behalf. Few contestants of any kind disregard the press. In short, those who pursue political stakes and prizes seldom operate entirely alone, and the world of politics, therefore, turns into an intricate network of alliances as each participant seeks support from others.

These alliances are far from permanent. Coalitions formed in connection with one issue often dissolve promptly when another comes up, and mutual supporters may turn into bitter opponents. One sees this tendency particularly in the parties, where factions will stand solidly together and praise one another one day, then denounce one another later on, only to reconcile their differences when solidarity again becomes crucial. The same situation applies to other alliances, too. Teachers' groups that endorse school superintendents' requests for more money for schools may be pitted against the superintendents over pay increases. Merchants' organizations and automobile associations may join to urge improvement of public-parking facilities, but may split over the desirability of one-way streets. Commuters second railroad requests for public assistance, but condemn their proposals for decreased service and increased fares. The web of relationships shifts constantly, and everyone knows that concessions made to someone today are not likely to remain binding for any length of time. They also learn that obligations run in both directions, so that a supporter who is an invaluable asset at one time may become a demanding burden and a political liability later on. As a result, wariness marks many coalitions, and all are formed with an understanding that expedience will probably take precedence over principle during the life of the entente.

100

Political Strategies

Nevertheless, subject to all these qualifications and tacit agreements, the search for, and the conditional granting of, support is one of the chief strategies of all who attempt to influence policy.

It is not always possible to persuade or induce other participants to do voluntarily what one wants them to do. In such cases a different strategy is usually introduced: getting them to do what one wants regardless of their own preferences by making any other course of action too costly for them to follow. When reason and the carrot fail, the stick falls.

Withdrawing or withholding support is probably the mildest of the sanctions, yet even this tactic can be damaging. A non-governmental group trying to block a program under consideration, or to promote a program that arouses anxiety or hostility in official circles, may find itself utterly disarmed if it cannot mobilize allies, particularly if the opposition is more successful in mobilizing *its* friends. A department trying to embark on a new policy, or to construct a new facility, may find itself blocked by pockets of resistance unless it can summon up proof of more widespread sympathy and approval. A political party may be seriously hampered if its donors and workers, let alone its voters, desert it at a critical moment.

But the penalties exacted from uncooperative fellow-participants by other participants are frequently severer than these passive measures, and are more aggressively imposed. For they can harass—by exposing questionable acts, by public criticism, by insistent complaint. Officials, bureaucrats, and party leaders are especially vulnerable to these tactics, for most of us seem to demand of them a higher standard of morality than we tolerate in others. What many businessmen do as a matter of course in the conduct of their enterprise, for example, might cost a public officer his job, his reputation, and perhaps his liberty. Moreover, the protections against defamation and libel tend to be somewhat less secure for political personalities than for others, so political figures are often subjected to attacks, without recourse, that would promptly be answered by lawsuits if directed against private citizens. It is perhaps not difficult to make a strong case for such differential ethical requirements, but that is not the point here. The fact is, public officers and employees, and party functionaries, too, are especially vulnerable to this kind of punishment.

This area is where the press, the reformers, and civic groups find their choicest opportunities. Newspapers thrive on civic scandals, and their reporters and editors in many places (especially in big cities) love to ferret them out. Civic groups sometimes conduct their own private investigations, and, with the aid of the press, spread their findings and charges before the community, the state, and even the nation if the accusations are sufficiently sensational. Occasionally, a single indignant and dedicated man will embark on a personal crusade. But more specialized organizations can also be devastating. A health department denounced by a medical society; a school system ridiculed by professional educators; a traffic plan assailed by motorists, truckers, bus companies, and merchants; and roads censured by highway engineers, for example, may severely embarrass an entire administration as well as the persons directly involved. 101

Political Strategies

Officials, bureaucrats, and parties may be hit from every side. Awareness of this risk impels most of them to avoid provocation if they can.

On the other hand, they, too, can inflict penalties on other participants. Officials can adopt laws and regulations, or institute investigations and legal proceedings, inimical to individuals or groups who have injured them. Bureaucrats can insist on the most punctilious observation of every provision of the law, and prosecute every violation, however minor. Both officials and bureaucrats can be more receptive to the competitors and opponents of those who attack them than to the attackers. Parties can utilize their access to government leaders to encourage retaliation against their adversaries. They sometimes succeed in diverting all public expenditures and contracts from opponents, and in pursuing fiscal policies their opponents abhor. By the same token, officials, bureaucrats, and parties occasionally get into disputes with one another. Officials may use their authority to discipline and penalize bureaucrats; bureaucrats may condemn "political interference" by officials and may drag their feet in executing directives, or may even strike;[10] party leaders may withhold nominations or conduct half-hearted election campaigns; officials may discharge appointees representing factions of the parties with which they are feuding, and so on. In short, no one is defenseless against others who play for the stakes of politics.

As you might suspect, sometimes these instruments of influence are abused. Just as bribery is an illicit reward offered public officeholders to induce them to accommodate a special interest, so officeholders may use their official powers to extract special considerations from other groups on pain of failing to do, or delaying, what they are charged to do. They may even try to exclude opponents from the ballot or the polls. And influential non-governmental groups may threaten to raise a hue and cry even when officeholders are merely performing their sworn duties; controversies can hurt officeholders even when they are innocent of wrongdoing, so they may be tempted to bow before such threats. Whatever can be used, in other words, can also be misused.

Violence must therefore be included in any catalogue of modes of political action. It was not very long ago that flying squads of thugs were employed by political rings, occasionally with the tacit connivance of the police, to intimidate voters in some large cities. Changing times, however, realignment of political forces, and redistributions of political strength have virtually wiped out this practice. In some parts of the South, on the other hand, violence has long been and still is a way of keeping Negroes from exercising their rights. Sometimes committed clandestinely, sometimes openly but without police interference, sometimes by law-enforcement officers themselves (who then risk federal prosecution), acts of terror and violence drove southern Negroes out of every corner of the political arena. Yet even in this case, the Negroes devised a counterstrategy. Enlisting support in other areas and in many quarters of the

[10] See David Zyskind, *One Thousand Strikes of Government Employees* (New York: Columbia University Press, 1940). Even where strikes of public employees are forbidden by statutes, they occur. In 1962, for example, a large number of teachers in New York City struck in a quest for higher pay, although a state statute prohibited strikes in the public service. No action was taken against them when the strike was settled.

Political Strategies

South itself, they have resorted to the federal courts, Congress, and to passive and non-violent methods of pressure, all of which are gradually readmitting them to the political process and will eventually restore to them their full and proper voice in the governments of the states and localities in which they reside.

One of the factors that helps prevent these broadly dispersed capacities to punish from degenerating into internecine warfare is widespread tolerance and fellow feeling. Most people are not out to destroy everyone else, not even their opponents. Equally important, though, is the fact that no one is immune from retaliation by others, and this vulnerability is a check on their behavior. The system of checks and balances among the three branches of government, so dear to the authors of books on civics, is not confined to the internal functioning of government exclusively. It is a state of affairs that pervades the whole political and governmental process, and, for that matter, the whole of our society. For punishment is a strategy all are capable of prosecuting.

THE EXERCISE OF "SOVEREIGNTY"

Officials and bureaucrats of the state governments can, in their relations with the localities, use all the strategies we have mentioned plus one more: the legal powers of states over local governments. All local units of government derive their authority from the states, and can exercise only so much as the state governments delegate to them (subject, of course, to the state constitutions). Considerable influence may be brought to bear on local governments via this channel, and even when state personnel may not themselves be inclined to apply leverage, they may find themselves under pressure from contestants who have had little luck at the local level but are able to muster greater strength at the state level for one reason or another. Consequently, this channel is extensively used.

The modes of influence are varied. The states can restrict the discretion of localities by limited grants of power (which remain quite inelastic because of "Dillion's Rule"). They can issue mandates to local officers, directing and requiring them to take specific actions under specified conditions and spelling out the way the actions are to be performed. Using their power over public finance throughout their jurisdiction, the states can reserve to themselves the best sources of revenues, and then distribute the money in the form of grants-in-aid to localities. Since almost one-fourth of all local revenues come from this source, local governments are in no position to reject many such grants and thus to escape the bestowal conditions imposed. These conditions may require local officials to obtain prior state approval before taking action in particular fields. Or the state may insist on the right of review of local activities, not only through routine reports, which abound, but by establishing lines of appeal from local officials to state officials, and by state investigations of local affairs (sometimes conducted by legislative bodies, sometimes by chief executives, sometimes by administrative officers, sometimes by special commissions). Moreover, many local officers are subject to removal by state authorities.

States usually exert influence on local governments through the medium of state statutes. In their conduct of the most familiar and important of public functions, most local officials and employees are actually administering state statutes rather than carrying out the provisions of locally adopted law, and the statutes are often very long and very detailed. The appropriate state administrative agencies generally maintain particularly close surveillance of localities to see that they adhere to the extensive state laws governing education, health, and welfare; and in these fields local agencies find themselves bound by abundant state administrative regulations as well as by legislation. It is in these functions, too, that grants,[11] prior approval, and review are most extensively and continuously employed, although the techniques are not at all foreign to other functions. Constitutional provisions, and executive and judicial intervention, tend to be less sweeping and continuous, but by no means negligible.

The federal government has not intervened in state or local government on nearly so broad a front as the states have intervened in local affairs. To be sure, the growth of federal programs has displaced or overshadowed state activity in some fields, and the prospect of such expansion may sometimes convince state officials that they ought to take action in order to forestall the need for federal action. But where the federal government has not actually taken over the dominant role in a function, its chief method of influencing state and local action has been through the grant-in-aid (chiefly for highways and welfare).[12] Recent court actions, federal laws, and executive action under court decisions and under the statutes, have underscored a long-established but newly invigorated type of federal intervention—the defense of federally protected rights of individuals under the Fourteenth Amendment. In addition, federal officers may find themselves involved willy-nilly in state or local affairs simply in conducting their ordinary business; highway and airport location, and radio and television station licenses, for example, may become local causes-célèbres from which federal officials may not be able to extricate themselves. But federal control of the states and localities is not nearly as pervasive as is state control of local governments.

In particular, direct relations between Washington and localities have been circumscribed; the states have traditionally resisted fiercely any intrusion between themselves and their subdivisions. Small grants have gone directly from the federal treasury to local governments for education, housing and community development, airports, and sewage-treatment facilities, and urban areas have tried with mixed results to use this straw in the wind as a way of forcing the states to show greater concern for cities. Nevertheless, direct contact and direct intervention from Washington is the exception rather than the rule.

Local authorities have established strategic defenses to control intervention in their affairs. They rally around the home-rule banner to fend off state officials. Their delegates in the state legislatures and in Congress speak for them. They remind officers with statewide constituencies of the need to win local support. Their administrative officials and executives appear in state capitols and in Washington to lobby. So they are not helpless. But the capacity of local officers to influence higher governmental

[11] See Table 10.
[12] *Ibid.*

Political Strategies

levels is still distinctly more restricted than the capacity of the states to influence local decisions and actions.

Consequently, many local participants in politics, defeated by the local configuration of forces, turn to other levels of government, and especially to the states, to seek redress. Since the political context in which their arguments are heard will ordinarily be quite different at the higher levels, with an altogether different pattern of alliances and hostilities and of strengths and weaknesses, a local setback is not necessarily an irremediable frustration; it is possible to triumph in the larger arena after suffering defeat in the smaller. Moreover, higher governmental levels, and most particularly the states, have the legal power to reverse many decisions of the localities. The incentives to seek relief there, consequently, are very strong, and the use of state authority at the local level is for this reason a common phenomenon.

Of course, even without pressure from other participants, the officers and employees of state governments are generally inclined to exert influence on local governments. For one thing, they are often sincerely concerned about the quality of local services for which they feel responsible, and for which, indeed, they may be held responsible by the public. For another, when one party controls a state government and another party controls a local government, these partisan differences provide state officers with additional incentives to intervene at the local level. Thirdly, the traditional pattern of state-local relations is such that localities are compelled to return repeatedly to the state capitals for permission or power to act in certain areas, and for money, and it sometimes demands an extraordinary degree of self-denial for men who have such power over others willingly to relinquish it. So, close state supervision of localities is likely to remain the norm for a long time.

The network of forces behind the use of compulsory powers by the states is thus complicated. But one thing is clear: as long as the present relationships among levels of government obtain, officials and employees at higher governmental levels, for reasons of their own and also because of pressure from other participants in state and local politics, will employ this strategy as one of the ways to influence the sharing of political rewards.

CREATING MYTHS AND IMPRESSIONS

Much of the time, it is almost as important to make other participants *believe* you have the means of applying all these strategies as it is actually to possess that capacity. In politics as in poker, bluffing is a vital strategy.

Hence the claim by so many contestants to speak for massive numbers of voters. Do ethnic-group leaders, religious leaders, the heads of veterans groups, and labor leaders actually "deliver" the votes of their memberships? In fact, do district leaders really carry their districts, or do they just claim credit for what would have happened anyway? Do newspapers and other mass media have such an impact on the public that they can sway an election? The evidence tends to be ambiguous rather than probative, but few persons in political life are willing to put these claims to rigid tests when so much is at stake. On the whole, it is often easier to try to placate these contestants than to risk the consequences of challenging them. So the world of government and politics includes many people who strive to establish the impression that their support is more valuable, and their retribution more terrible, than it may actually be.

A related but distinguishable strategy is the creation of a public image beyond reproach and above suspicion. The other party's (or faction's) chief is a "boss," and his following "a machine"; one's own chief is a "leader," and one's own following "an organization." (Modern party leaders tend to present themselves to the public as ordinary "organization men," just like corporation executives simply trying to run an orderly shop. They would apparently like to slough off the liabilities of identification with the nineteenth-century urban politician.) It is often effective, too, to don the mantle of the "reformer." Administrators and bureaucracies decry as "politics" every attempt by elected and high appointed officials to influence their behavior, ascribing to themselves and their specialized constituencies a selfless devotion to the commonweal that makes every opponent and critic either an uninformed fool or a malicious knave. (The practitioners of the professions, even including some city managers, are especially prone to this technique, but the symptoms are not confined to them exclusively.) Special districts and special authorities raise the same cry, contending that only expertness and efficiency motivate them, and that their critics are driven by misconceptions and evil intentions. Politicians and other residents of rural sections and small towns proclaim their areas the citadels of piety and purity, and denounce cities and industry as breeders of sin and wickedness (thereby justifying in their own minds the underrepresentation of urban and industrial areas in many state governments). Some men, in government and out, project an image of "incorruptible" statesmen, immune to the lures that tempt lesser persons, and therefore entitled to special attention and deference and perhaps even to the highest public offices. (This posture is a particular advantage of the rich.) Another public "type" is the man of action, who speaks bluntly and even acidly, "gets things done," has no patience with long-range planners and others who would pause to assess the costs as well as the benefits of proposed innovations and great public works, cows his opposition, and points to his trail of accomplishments as monuments to his ability and proof of his genius. Those who are able to establish such images of themselves and their organizations are ordinarily able to affect the formulation and execution of public policy much more profoundly than any objective evaluation of their other sources of strength would indicate is possible.

In these strategies as in so many of the others, the mass media of communication are cast in a key role. To be sure, they cannot accomplish miracles; they cannot indefinitely conceal ineptitude, dishonesty, and negligence when day-by-day performance betrays these failings, nor can they create an aura of corruption and mismanagement when the facts persistently point the other way, particularly in larger governmental jurisdictions where there are *many* newspapers and periodicals and radio and television stations covering the news. Still, the way each participant looks to all the others, to the electorate, and perhaps even to himself, is deeply colored by the attitude of the mass media. Like radio announcers reporting on sporting events their audiences cannot see, the mass media can portray some contestants as exciting and dramatic, others as drab and suspect, and the portrayal might well surprise people who actually see the contests.

Political Strategies

It takes time for corrective information to come through other channels (but, in a diversified society like ours, it does come eventually).

It is not within the reach of every participant to bluff successfully or to establish a noble image. Indeed, there are hazards in these tactics. A single bluff discovered may lead to distrust for a long time afterward and to repeated tests of power that can wear a contestant down. A single slip by a man or a group surrounded by a glow of perfection may be enough to disillusion everyone who believed in them, to destroy the image so painstakingly built up, while the same lapse on the part of a lesser participant would occasion no notice. Yet such are the advantages of enjoying a reputation that persuades others to listen, to heed, and to raise no doubts, that many seek it and a surprising number achieve it.

A RICHNESS OF WEAPONS

Looking back over the discussion of the nature of the federal system, the structure of state and local government, the dimensions and variety of the prizes and rewards to be gained by participating in the governmental process, the many kinds of participants and their different positions in the process, and the endless opportunities to exercise influence at one point in the process even if one is thwarted at half a dozen others, we might conclude that the profusion of strategies and tactics for applying such leverage is a natural—indeed, an inevitable—outgrowth of the political environment. At any rate, multiformity is certainly the outstanding characteristic of the means of influence at the disposal of political participants. And these weapons are employed with vigor and imagination.

The Political Plexus

Virtually every decision or action that emerges from this plethora of contending forces represents a compromise, a more-or-less enduring settlement of differences and competing claims. What happens in the government and politics of our states and localities is the product of myriad bargains and concessions, with negotiations never ceasing, although they vary in intensity from place to place and from time to time. The process might be described as decision by mutual accommodation.

The calculus of compromise is often exceedingly complex. A group makes a demand on a party for a place on the ticket at election. Although the demand may be denied, an appointment later on—perhaps as an aide to the candidate selected, perhaps in another department entirely, perhaps in another branch of government, maybe even in a different level of government altogether—may appease the offended claimants. A participant in the political contest is antagonized by the rejection of his recommendations for governmental reorganization, but may be placated by the selection of men to operate the old machinery who seem likely to conduct the government in much the way the reorganization was intended to encourage. An outcry for new legislation may result in more rigorous enforcement of old laws, with the same effect. Thus ostensible defeats may be transformed into *de facto* victories by accommodations reached in other places or at other times.

107

Political Strategies

By the same token, surface victories may be won at heavy real cost. A group whose demands for representation are satisfied may find it difficult to attack unpopular policies for which its representatives must share responsibility. A reorganized system or agency or party may turn out to be indistinguishable from its predecessors if manned by the same kind of personnel, yet the advocates of reorganization may find their momentum dissipated by the initial victory, and embarrassed to seek office themselves lest their opponents insist that personal gain was their actual objective in advocating change. A piece of controversial legislation is guided through a hazardous course to enactment, but the price of passage is extensive amendment; the amenders then take credit for enacting a courageous response to a pressing problem, and the disappointed originators fear to criticize their own brainchild despite its emasculation lest they destroy even its remnants. It would therefore be a mistake to look for an immediate *quid pro quo* in connection with each bargain. The network is farflung and intricate; the strategists are ingenious; the arrangements they make are subtle and complicated.

The complications are amplified by what has been called "the rule of anticipated reactions."[13] What the participants do is based partly on their estimates of what others will do. They may support a candidate they dislike because they are more afraid of his punitive powers should he win than they are of the ability of his opponents to punish should the opponents succeed. (Some non-governmental groups make it a point to contribute to both major parties in order to maintain lines of access no matter who is victorious.) They may decide not to push for a program they favor because they think it will stimulate a great many latent groups to take concerted action to defeat it. They may resist a reorganization in which they have no direct interest, because they hope it will facilitate winning support later on for issues they *do* care about. Officials and bureaucrats may adopt a policy of lax enforcement of laws they know will be violated wholesale (such as some speed laws, parking regulations, Sunday closing laws for businesses, and so-called "blue laws"). In other words, what comes out of the machinery of state and local government is a function not only of agreements explicitly reached but also of expectations about future understandings, of obligations incurred in the past, and of anxieties about upsetting existing arrangements. The close student of political affairs learns to look for the inarticulate premises of decision and action as well as the explicit and visible ones.

This complex pattern of interactions determines what our state and local governments are and do (and the federal government, too, since state and local jurisdictions are, as we saw, such prominent elements of the federal system). The whole thing sometimes seems too complicated to permit any meaningful generalization to be made. Is it possible to do anything more profound by study and analysis than observe that every decision and every action should be viewed against a backdrop of numerous factors intricately interwoven with one another? To this question we turn in the next, the concluding, chapter.

[13] First employed by Carl J. Friedrich; see his *Constitutional Government and Democracy* (Boston: Little, Brown, 1941), pp. 589–591. See also, Herbert A. Simon, *Administrative Behavior* (New York: Macmillan, 1947), pp. 129 f., 234.

Political Strategies

State
and Local
Government
in Perspective

Islands of Decision

If every strategy of every political contestant
in every state and locality had to be formulated with every other
contestant in mind, no one could make any plans or make
any moves on anything remotely resembling a rational basis.
What makes it feasible for them to make their calculations with a fair
degree of accuracy is that most calculations need
take into account only a limited segment of the web,

for this is all that is relevant to the specific political stakes in which most contestants are interested. To know the general attributes of the whole system is to perceive more clearly the way it operates in its specifics, but all the elements of the entire system need not be considered *in toto* to describe and assess each individual situation. Most state governments, and probably most local governments, are not monolithic entities. Rather, each consists of a complex of decision-making "islands." From each such island emanates a flow of decisions and actions embodying the stakes and prizes of politics. The flow from any given island is only loosely related to the flow from all the others; all are, by the same token, relatively autonomous.

Every island is composed of a cluster of participants especially concerned with the types of decision that issue from it, and includes all categories of participants and all the varieties of participation that share that common interest. All the participants in each cluster do not wield equal influence, and their strength tends to vary from decision to decision. Those persons authorized to announce official decisions or take official action—to legitimize them by signature—ordinarily occupy key positions in any cluster, and constitute what may be called "core groups"; the other members rotate around them trying to influence the contents of the issuances, and thus may be designated "satellite groups." The core groups, however, are not always, or even most of the time, the total masters of any cluster. Although their position is by definition central, it is the interaction of core and satellite groups that produces most decisions. Each constellation lives and works for the most part in a world of its own, largely unconcerned with what goes on in other areas except as these developments impinge on its own central interests.[1]

In matters involving nominations, party leaders tend to be the core groups. For appointments, the core groups are appointing officers. For elections, everyone is satellite to the electorate. For all other decisions officials are the core groups, especially officials with specialized functions (education, police, health, welfare, and so on), but also officials of the general · institutions of government (legislature, executive, judiciary). Around each of these groups collect the other participants bent on influencing what the core groups do. (We should mention in passing that the core group of one constellation may appear as a satellite group in another.)

The whole pattern of governmental activities, policies, programs, and functions in our states and localities is a product of the combined flows from all these islands. Each affects some others in some ways, but the overall configuration is not a deliberately engineered design nor are all the parts fully articulated. There is little central direction in any real sense.

Again, let us emphasize that this pattern is not equally applicable to all states and all localities.[2] In many a small community the range of governmental activities is narrow, and the population and economic base are too small and too undifferentiated to sustain a large array of specialized non-governmental groups and several competing newspapers. Consequently, there are fewer occasions for bargaining in the political arena, and interactions may be personal rather than institutional or collective. Yet

[1] Wallace S. Sayre and Herbert Kaufman, *Governing New York City* (New York: Russell Sage Foundation, 1960), Chapter XIX.
[2] Cf., pp. 19–20, 86–87.

State and Local Government in Perspective

even in such communities, we may surmise, similar processes doubtless occur because no population is completely homogeneous, and the interplay among the seekers of the stakes and prizes of political action probably constitutes a microcosm of the more elaborately developed regions, with individuals performing the roles played by organizations in more populous jurisdictions. For cities of even moderate size, the description outlined here is probably much more accurate. In the largest metropolises it may be quite precise. Likewise, in the less populous states, it may apply only with substantial qualifications (although politics at the state level everywhere is probably closer to the model than to the exceptional simplicity of the rural community), whereas for the large industrial states the model probably is a reasonably faithful portrayal of the governmental process.

At bottom, the governmental process is only a reflection of the basic social characteristics of a political community. The finer the division of labor, the gradations of wealth, and the status distinctions, the greater the variety of organizations and associations, of perspective and value, of objectives and methods of pursuing them. The early ideal of undifferentiated citizens jointly partaking in all the decisions and responsibilities of government was probably a misreading of conditions even when it was propounded, but it certainly is seldom, if ever, approximated today. In greater or lesser degree, numerous islands of political decision are doubtless to be found in every body politic, but they are more conspicuous in the economically advanced ones. Whether this difference in degree is so great as to constitute a difference in kind cannot be determined precisely until we have more comparative data.

The Problem of State and Local Elites

From all that we have said, it follows that state or local governments dominated by a small cohesive clique, or even by a single category of participants, are probably a small minority of the total. Assuredly, they are not unknown; there are still "company towns," and states (like Montana) where "the company" (Anaconda Copper, in this case) cuts an overwhelming figure in the economy, the social life, and on the political stage.[3] Even in these cases, however, the advent of unions and the growth of anti-company sentiment outside the ranks of the company leadership have made it possible to challenge the monopoly of the companies, if not to break it. Elsewhere, the "old families" have similarly been compelled to bargain with newer elements of society—industrialists, commercial interests, aggressive farm groups, new residents, the professions and skilled trades, new real-estate developers, politically awakening minorities, and others—no longer content to accept the principles of aristocracy and oli-

[3] Cf., John Gunther, *Inside U. S. A.* (New York: Harper, 1947), pp. 166–174. See also, generally, Robert Engler, *The Politics of Oil* (New York: Macmillan, 1961), and especially the statement of the chairman of the Texas Democratic State Executive Committee in 1947 that "the oil industry is in complete control of state politics and state government," quoted on p. 354. Harold J. Laski, in *The American Democracy* (New York: Viking, 1948), makes similar observations about the DuPonts in Delaware (p. 148), but Gunther (p. 634) disputes this. Laski also observes, however, that complete domination of a state by a single vested interest is exceptional (p. 148).

garchy once regarded as the norm.[4] If here and there a comparatively stable coalition of several powerful elements manages to hold sway over the government and politics of a community, it is fairly unusual, and maneuvering, negotiation, and compromising may well take place inside the coalition much as they do on the larger scene in more open communities.

Still, the question is not closed. Many community studies continue to report the existence of ruling elites.[5] Yet voices of dissent and criticism are heard increasingly. Meanwhile, the evidence of elites continues to come from fairly small communities; in larger and more diversified places, the multi-centered system of decision "islands" doubtless obtains.

This condition at least casts serious doubt on the allegations of some observers that state and local officials, bureaucrats, and party leaders are everywhere nothing more than tools of a fairly cohesive ruling "business" group.[6] It also runs contrary to the notion that a handful of party "bosses" run entire states and localities by themselves, with no one able to resist or oppose them effectively.[7] Indeed, the highest governmental and party officials may be *used* as instruments by a constellation of specialized interest groups and administrators and bureaucrats seeking action on some issue within their specialty more often than the officials themselves use these groups. We know surprisingly little about the tightly disciplined Byrd machine in Virginia, or about the growth of William F. Callahan's power in Massachusetts in recent years. We have seen the Long organization in

[4] See Robert A. Dahl, *Who Governs?* (New Haven: Yale University Press, 1961), Book I; Samuel Lubell, *The Future of American Politics* (New York: Harper, 1952), Chapter 3.

[5] A full review and analysis of the relevant literature may be found in Nelson W. Polsby, *Community Power and Political Theory* (unpublished doctoral dissertation, Yale University, 1961, soon to be published by the Yale University Press). Among the prominent studies of ruling elites cited by Polsby are Robert S. Lynd and Helen M. Lynd, *Middletown* (New York: Harcourt, Brace, 1929) and *Middletown in Transition* (New York: Harcourt, Brace, 1937); W. Lloyd Warner and Paul S. Lunt, *The Social Life of a Modern Community* (New Haven: Yale University Press, 1941) and *The Status System of a Modern Community* (New Haven: Yale University Press, 1942); E. Digby Baltzell, *Philadelphia Gentlemen* (Glencoe, Ill.: The Free Press, 1958); William Lloyd Warner, et al., *Democracy in Jonesville* (New York: Harper, 1949); August B. Hollingshead, *Elmtown's Youth* (New York: Wiley, 1949); Floyd Hunter, *Community Power Structure* (Chapel Hill: University of North Carolina Press, 1953); Delbert C. Miller, "Industry and Community Power Structure," *American Sociological Review*, Vol. 23, No. 1 (February, 1958), pp. 9 ff., and "Decision-making Cliques in Community Power Structures," *American Journal of Sociology*, Vol. 64, No. 3 (November, 1958), pp. 299 ff.

[6] See, for example, Laski, *op. cit.*, Chapter IV; David Lynch, *The Concentration of Economic Power* (New York: Columbia University Press, 1946), pp. 293–300; D. W. Brogan, *Government of the People* (New York: Harper, 1943, new ed.), pp. 260–295. See also, the works cited in Note 5.

[7] Perhaps the most impassioned statement of this point of view was that of Elihu Root in an oft-quoted speech to the New York State constitutional convention of 1915. "What is the government of this state?" he asked. "What has it been during the forty years of my acquaintance with it? The government of the constitution? Oh, no; not half the time, nor half way. . . . From the days of Fenton, and Conkling, and Arthur, and Cornell, and Platt, from the days of David B. Hill, down to the present time, the government of the state has presented two different lines of activity, one of the constitution and the statutory offices of the state, and the other of the party leaders—they call them party bosses, they call the system . . . 'invisible government.' " Quoted in Howard R. Penniman, Sait's *American Parties and Elections*, 4th ed. (New York: Appleton-Century-Crofts, 1948), p. 357.

State and Local Government in Perspective

Louisiana, the Roraback organization in Connecticut, the Hague empire in New Jersey, the Crump machine in Tennessee, and the Pendergast machine in Missouri, among others, suffer grievous splits, if not utter disintegration, during the past generation. Yet why these organizations collapsed remains something of a mystery. We have yet to find out whether, while the organizations functioned, their leaders crushed and subdued all potential opposition, on the one hand, or won it over to their side, on the other. If the former, was it the result of nothing more than the charismatic personality of the leader who lends his name to the movement? Or is there something special about states and localities in which such machines develop that generates and nurtures the machines? If the leaders simply succeeded in winning over participants in the political contest, was their rule contingent on continuing to satisfy the claims of their manifold supporters, so that they were prisoners as well as rulers? Was their influence as all-pervasive as it was made out to be (by themselves, in order to foster the legend of invincibility, as well as by others), or were they merely particularly strong in some decision-making island that received greater attention than others in which they took little part? To these queries, there are as yet no definitive answers; the problem of state and local elites remains open. The best guess is that allegedly close-knit governing cliques will turn out to be far less unified in fact than in myth.

Low Integration and Its Consequences

WEAKNESS OF THE SYSTEM

A political system characterized by numerous decision centers entails grave risks, for it facilitates deadlock, delay, and obstruction. As long as every proposal and every innovation must run a gantlet, the system is loaded against change. With so many participants possessing a veto, it encourages obstruction. When the fate of every measure turns on concessions to hosts of claimants, action is apt to come slowly and to be considerably adulterated. This situation can be costly, even hazardous, in time of great stress.

Moreover, a system that reaches decisions by accommodation and compromise may move by drift rather than by direction. There are times when it can afford this luxury; there are other times when concerted, deliberate action is required. Nothing in such a fragmented system guarantees direction; no one can be sure of either leadership or consensus on a desirable course when necessary. Conceivably, a state or a locality could drift into situations nobody wants, and get so deeply enmeshed that only the most drastic measures could extricate them, if anything could.

Finally, the special, narrow perspectives of each separate constellation of forces often outweigh any broader considerations involving common interests of all the participants in all the islands of decision. Those groups with a broad range of interests are reduced to merely one among a number of specialized contestants whenever they enter any specialized arena, and their influence may be counterbalanced and even offset by the aggregates of influence the special interests can mobilize. Thus, broader premises of decision and action may be drowned out by the volume and intensity of narrow premises.

113

Of course, political systems in which a single group dominates do not always escape these weaknesses. After all, a ruling clique hostile to change can be far more obstructionist than a large number of political participants, each armed with the resources and strategies we have already discussed. And a single hesitant, indecisive ruler can leave a polity even more helplessly adrift than many interacting groups are likely to. Furthermore, a clique or a single dominant person tends to confuse its (or his) own interests with the well-being of all, thus neglecting whatever common interests may be involved. So the weaknesses of the multi-centered politics of our states and localities are not unique to our kind of politics; they may crop up anywhere, and persist indefinitely because there is nothing to check or reverse them.

What is more, it is not at all clear that these logical shortcomings actually afflict our state and local governments. As we have seen, these governments have been exceedingly inventive and flexible with regard to organization and procedure. They have also risen dramatically to the challenges of the post-World War II world, increasing their expenditures and their functions at a far faster rate than the federal government has expanded its non-war budget and activities. This is not the type of behavior we associate with governments that are paralyzed, directionless, and unguided. In spite of the hazards, our state and local jurisdictions have been vigorous, adaptive, and creative.

Here, the difference between the exceptional receptivity to change on the part of the larger states and the cities as against more rural areas comes strikingly to the fore. We mentioned in an earlier chapter that many rural areas still cling to forms identified with earlier eras, whereas urban states and cities have experimented continuously with structural and procedural arrangements. Moreover, the range of governmental services in the less industrialized sections, and sometimes the public expenditures per capita, are rarely equal to the services performed and expenditures disbursed in more industrialized areas. One reason is that the industrialized areas can *afford* more service, but equally important is the fact that they have political systems in which people can *demand* and *get* more service.

For one of the consequences of the loose-jointed, diffuse politics of states and localities is the ability of each constellation of participants to push ahead in the areas it considers important. The cluster of groups in public health advocate improving and expanding public-health programs. Corresponding movements develop in the welfare field, and in highways, education, fire and police protection, and in all the other fields of governmental action. Now on one front, now on another, a coalition of contestants breaks through with something new. Each innovation compels adjustments in related fields, and these adjustments, in turn, force changes in the fields *they* overlap. So the system is constantly in flux—and precisely *because* of the very diffusion that also can mire it down. The diversity in industrial areas multiplies these stimuli exponentially.

Another advantage in having a multiplicity of decision centers in most of our states and almost all our cities is the opportunities it affords

State and Local Government in Perspective

every group to defend what it considers to be its interests. Such an arrangement provides broad access to officials and insures every participant an opportunity to extract concessions.

Again, the more varied the participants, the greater the opportunities. Here is one of the reasons why the exclusion of minorities from the political process—Negroes in the South, Mexican-Americans in the Southwest, Indians in the mountain states—has been more systematic in the least industrialized and urban parts of the country, and why even in those regions the minorities have begun to score limited but impressive advances in the cities. Not that minorities find paradise in the large cities and large states. But they have found their political footholds there, and they are beginning to make good use of them—in local government, in state government, and in Washington. And other less-handicapped participants in state and local politics have shown them the way by demonstrating that no one need tolerate his own exclusion from the decision-making process.

The Delicate Balance

Thus the defects of our system of state and local government are in many ways the sources of its accomplishments and proudest claims; its strengths are at the same time the source of its greatest dangers. The future will test sternly the capacity of our state and local governments to meet its challenges. Will the governments of those states and localities that embrace many decision centers bog down and collapse under the burdens that the second half of the twentieth century will surely thrust on them, or will they gradually sacrifice the benefits of their diffuseness in order to achieve forceful direction? On the other hand, will the states and localities in which there are few decision centers display the flexibility and inventiveness that the years ahead will call for, or will they cling stubbornly to creaking machinery, outmoded concepts, old prejudices?

It would be nice to be able to conclude this little volume with a burst of Fourth-of-July oratory, full of confidence and optimism and good cheer because there can be no doubt that everything will turn out for the best in the end. But the challenges will be great, the tests severe, and the outcome by no means an assured and automatic victory. Yet the difficulties of the task, the dangers and hardships in following the course we have charted for our state governments, our localities, and even for the federal system as a whole, need neither discourage nor depress us. On the contrary, they should exhilarate us, for men have seldom embarked on such a political adventure as we, every day, are called upon to experience. Whether we attain the goals we have set depends not on international politics alone. Our survival will be decided in the international arena, but the *kind* of lives we lead will be determined very substantially at the state and local levels. At these levels, as at the national and international levels, the issue is in doubt. Battles of this kind have to be fought anew every day. The situation should not be cause for pessimism, but for excitement, and even for gratification, because to continue fighting these battles is to remain free.

To Explore Further . . .

All a brief review of this kind can do effectively is to suggest where a student can find material relevant to his own interests. To begin with, the student will find most helpful the following selected bibliographies:

Governmental Affairs Foundation, Inc., *Metropolitan Communities: a Bibliography, with Special Emphasis on Government and Politics* (Chicago: Public Administration Service, 1956). *Supplement: 1955–1957* (Chicago: Public Administration Service, 1960.)

Norman Meller, "Legislative Behavior Research," *Western Political Quarterly,* Vol. XIII, No. 1 (March, 1960), pp. 131–153.

State Government: an Annotated Bibliography (Chicago: Council of State Governments, 1959. Revised periodically.)

Government Affairs Foundation, Inc., *Metropolitan Surveys: a Digest* (Chicago: Public Administration Service, 1958.)

Robert T. Daland, "Political Science and the Study of Urbanism," *The American Political Science Review,* Vol. LI, No. 2 (June, 1957), pp. 491–509.

U.S. Library of Congress. Legislative Reference Service. *Inter-Governmental Relations in the United States: a Selected Bibliography,* prepared for the Intergovernmental Relations Subcommittee of the Committee on Government Operations of the House of Representatives, 84th Cong., 2d Sess. (Washington, D.C.: Government Printing Office, 1956). This is a revision of U.S. Commission on Intergovernmental Relations, *Intergovernmental Relations in the United States: a Selected Bibliography* (mimeo., 1955).

Dorothy Tomkins, *State Government and Administration: A Bibliography* (Berkeley: University of California, Bureau of Public Administration, 1954).

Federal-State-Local Relations: a Selected Bibliography, prepared by the Joint Reference Library for the American Municipal Association and the Council of State Governments (Chicago: Joint Reference Library, 1954).

J. Alton Burdine, "Basic Materials for the Study of State Constitutions and State Constitutional Development," *The American Political Science Review,* Vol. XLVIII, No. 4 (December, 1954), pp. 1140–1152.

W. Brooke Graves, Norman J. Small, and E. Foster Dowell, *American State Government: a State by State Bibliography* (Chicago: Council of State Governments, 1948).

Marianne Yates and Martha Gilchrist, *Administrative Reorganization of State Governments: a Bibliography* (Chicago: Council of State Governments, 1948).

There are also bibliographies for some states and regions, as, for example:

State and Local Government in Illinois: a Bibliography (Urbana: University of Illinois, Institute of Government and Public Affairs, 1953 and 1958).

Bibliography on State and Local Government in New England (Boston University, Bureau of Public Administration, 1952).

Bibliographies on individual governmental functions (e.g., health, education, welfare, planning, civil service) may contain additional references of immediate interest and applicability. Textbooks on state and local government often contain short lists of both general and specialized books and articles, and textbooks and collections of readings in urban sociology provide valuable background material. And at virtually every state university there is a bureau of government research whose unpublished papers, studies, and reports supply information not easily accessible elsewhere.

Articles, book reviews, and surveys of recent writing and research appear in a number of journals and other periodicals: *The American Political Science Review, The Annals of the American Academy of Political and Social Science, The Journal of Politics, Metropolitan Area Problems, The Midwest Journal of Political Science, National Civic Review, Political Science Quarterly, Public Administration Review, Public Management, State Government, State Government News, U.S. Municipal News,* and *Western Political Quarterly.* Most are indexed in the Public Affairs Information Service's Annual *Bulletin.*

Two standard reference works that are particularly useful for the student of state and local government are *The Book of the States* and *The Municipal Year Book.*

Case studies provide insights into the processes of state and local government that more extensive surveys and general treatments cannot. A number may be found in the pioneer collection, Harold Stein (ed.), *Public Administration and Policy Development* (New York: Harcourt, Brace, 1952), which was followed by an even larger list of studies individually published from time to time by The Inter-University Case Program (University, Alabama: University of Alabama Press). The Eagleton Institute of Politics has produced another series, Studies in Practical Politics, of which about fifteen have been published individually (New York: Holt, Rinehart and Winston) in the last few years. Other collections of cases are Richard T. Frost (ed.), *Cases in State and Local Government* (Englewood Cliffs, N.J.: Prentice-Hall, 1962); Warner E. Mills, Jr., and Harry R. Davis, *Small City Government: Seven Cases in Decision Making* (New York: Random House, 1962); Edwin A. Bock and Alan K. Campbell (eds.), *Case Studies in American Government* (New York: Prentice-Hall, 1962); and Alan F. Westin (ed.), *The Uses of Power: 7 Cases in American Politics* (New York: Harcourt, Brace & World, 1962). A new collection, edited by Edwin A. Bock, is scheduled to appear soon. Some theoretical analyses based on case studies are Roscoe C. Martin, Frank J. Munger, *et al., Decisions in Syracuse* (Bloomington: Indiana University Press, 1962); Edward C. Banfield, *Political Influence* (Glencoe, Ill.: The Free Press, 1961); Peter H. Rossi and Robert A. Dentler, *The Politics of Urban Renewal* (Glencoe, Ill.: The Free Press, 1961); Martin Meyerson and Edward C. Banfield, *Politics, Planning, and the Public Interest* (Glencoe, Ill.: The Free Press, 1955). See also Henry J. Schmandt, Paul G. Steinbicker, and George D. Wendel, *Metropolitan Reform in St. Louis: A Case Study* (New York: Holt, Rinehart and Winston, 1961).

Some community studies (see Note 5, p. 112, and Morris Janowitz (ed.), *Community Political Systems* (Glencoe, Ill.: The Free Press, 1961)) capture the flavor of political realities. Two recent intensive analyses of city government and politics are Robert A. Dahl, *Who Governs?* (New Haven: Yale University Press, 1961) and Wallace S. Sayre and Herbert Kaufman, *Governing New York City* (New York: Russell Sage Foundation, 1960).

For studies of politics in individual states, see Fred I. Greenstein, *The American Party System and the American People* (Englewood Cliffs, N.J.: Prentice-Hall, 1963) and Malcolm E. Jewell, *The State Legislature: Politics and Practices* (New York: Random House, 1962).

A student will be greatly assisted in consulting original sources if he first examines E. E. Schattschneider and Victor Jones, *Local Political Surveys* (New York: Holt, Rinehart and Winston, 1962); William Riker, *The Study of Local Politics* (New York: Random House, 1959); E. E. Schattschneider, Victor Jones, and Stephen K. Bailey, *A Guide to the Study of Public Affairs* (New York: Sloane, 1952); and Miles O. Price and Harry Bitner, *Effective Legal Research* (Boston: Little, Brown, 1953).

These sources will guide him into constitutions, charters, and the docu-

To Explore Further . . .

ments of constitutional conventions and charter commissions; into the statutes and ordinances; into the journals of legislatures, proceedings of city councils and other local legislative bodies, and the reports of their committees and councils and commissions; into the manuals and yearbooks issued by the states to summarize basic information about state government and current state officers; into the rules and regulations issued by state and local administrative officers; into court reports and reporters; and even into the rules of the political parties.

To compare jurisdictions, the student will find his task eased by Legislative Drafting Fund of Columbia University, *Index Digest of State Constitutions* (New York: Oceana, 1959), and by Council of State Governments, *Constitutional and Statutory Provisions of the States,* a series of bulletins summarizing constitutional and statutory provisions on various subjects, compiled by the Library of Congress and issued from time to time by the Council. The Library of Congress, through the Government Printing Office in Washington, issues a number of reports, including a *Monthly Checklist of State Publications* and a *State Law Index*. At the municipal level the publications of the National Institute of Municipal Law Officers (Washington, D.C.) facilitate comparison of legislation and litigation. The *Model State Constitution* and the *Model City Charter,* both issued by the National Municipal League furnish interesting contrasts to prevailing practice. *Proceedings of the Governors' Conference* (Chicago: The Governors' Conference) are issued annually.

Every governmental unit has a budget, or at least an appropriation act. The documents are not always easy to decipher, or to track down, but they are almost always revealing.

The federal government is an unmatched source of information, especially the Bureau of the Census, not only for its decennial *Census of Population,* but also for its special censuses (such as business, agriculture, housing), and particularly for its quintennial *Census of Governments* (the next one due in 1962), which contains a wide range of data about organization, finances, and other aspects of state and local governments. The Bureau of the Census also prepares *The County and City Data Book,* and a number of reports on metropolitan areas, including *Population of Standard Metropolitan Areas, Local Government in Standard Metropolitan Areas,* and the *Growth of Metropolitan Districts in the United States.* And its Governments Division regularly publishes reports on state and local finances and personnel not obtainable from any other source. The Bureau of Labor Statistics issues monthly statements on state and local government employment and payrolls; the Office of Area Development of the Department of Commerce issues an *Area Trend Series;* and the Legislative Reference Division of the Library of Congress is the origin of many relevant reports and studies, as are the documents and reports of the various federal agencies that administer grants to states and cities.

For more detailed information about selected individual cities, including statistics on electoral behavior, the reports of the Joint Center for Urban Studies of the Massachusetts Institute of Technology and Harvard University are most valuable. (For sources on elections and other statistical data, see Riker, *op. cit.,* pp. 111–126.)

Students also should consult *Public Administration Organizations: A Directory,* 7th ed. (Chicago: Public Administration Clearing House, 1954) for ideas on where to turn for research assistance. University bureaus of government research (or public administration) in each state are also among the most useful resources, because they concentrate on special area problems.

Despite the volume of written material available, a great deal of it is narrowly technical. So the challenge to the imaginative student, and the opportunities for bringing new insights and fresh ideas into our "natural laboratories," remain vast and exciting. The field has not been exhausted; its immense possibilities cry out for exploration by original minds.

To Explore Further . . .

Index